Stop Prolonging
Your Loved One's Addiction

*How Your 'Helping' May
Actually Be Hurting*

Jon R. Sorenson

Stop Prolonging Your Loved One's Addiction:
How Your 'Helping' May Actually Be Hurting

Copyright © 2020 Jon R. Sorenson
Printed in USA | First printing edition: 2020
ISBN: 978-0-578-72688-5 (Paperback)

Jon Sorenson, Author LLC
looa.faithbased@gmail.com
www.LovedOnesOfAddicts.org
www.facebook.com/groups/LOOAGroup

Author's Note:

As an independent Christian author, the writing of this book was based on my personal experience as the father of an alcoholic son, a support group facilitator to loved ones of addicts, the founder and leader of a church recovery group, and extensive professional research.

My recovery and support group experience is as a lay leader, not a counselor or pastor. As such, this book is not a substitute for the advice of health care professionals. Therefore, I encourage you, if needed, to consult with a qualified Christian counselor and/or pastor for added guidance.

All viewpoints and opinions expressed herein are my own. I have no affiliation with any organization or treatment program. All stories are true; none are fictionalized or composites.

May God use this book to help you avoid codependent behavior that negatively affects your life and prolongs your loved one's addiction.

Jon Sorenson, Author LLC

Contents

Dedication

To my son, Chris...

Over the years, addiction and codependency robbed us of many wonderful experiences and memories together—perhaps more due to my poor choices than yours.

But that is the past. Today we celebrate a renewed relationship based on mutual love, forgiveness, reconciliation, and trust. As such, we've become living testimonies of God's promise in Joel 2:25: *"I will repay you for the years the locusts have eaten"* (NIV).

This book would never have been possible without your transparency, vulnerability, and genuine desire to help others in situations similar to ours. For this selfless gesture, you have earned my lifelong respect and admiration.

I'm so proud of your sobriety and the person you've become. I will always be there for you—unconditionally. And I couldn't love you more than I already do.

Dad

Acknowledgements

- To my wife, Nancie, for recognizing my need for counseling when my codependency spiraled out of control, and for her unwavering love and encouragement to complete this project;

- To my daughter, Traci, who grew up wise beyond her years, and intuitively understood Chris's need for tough love and boundaries long before I did;

- To my stepdaughter, Melinda, for being so much like her mom—a constant source of patience and understanding when I needed it most;

- To my daughter-in-law, Jari, for looking past the ugliness of Chris's addiction to see the loving and compassionate man he truly is;

- To Chris's mother, Lynn, an ever-present source of strength and fortitude, who accompanied me on heartbreaking trips to ERs, jails, rehabs, and court hearings;

- To the staff and members of Grace Church in Eden Prairie, Minnesota, who faithfully prayed for Chris's sobriety;

- To Dr. David Mellberg and the amazing staff of Christian psychologists at Minnesota Psychological Resources, without whom my marriage would undoubtedly have ended and Chris's addiction would still be rampant;

- And to my Lord and Savior, Jesus Christ, whose constant love and abiding presence helped stop my enabling behavior, and the prolonging of Chris's addiction.

Introduction

How It Began

"Heading out," said Chris, my 17-year-old son, bolting through the living room on his way to meet friends.

Once out the door, my wife, Nancie (Chris's stepmother), said matter-of-factly, "He's been drinking alcohol. I can smell it." She was perceptive of such things, having previously foster-parented adolescents with addiction issues. But her words left me defiant.

"No way," I countered, trying not to sound overly defensive. Easy to do when one stepparent criticizes the other's child. "You're just smelling cologne or something."

Of course, I later confirmed I was right (sarcasm intended) when I confronted Chris on whether he'd been drinking earlier in the evening. His emphatic "No!" was good enough for me, and a huge relief. Whew! Case closed. Time to move on. Nothing to worry about.

Nothing, that was, until several weeks later when a hospital called to report Chris was in their ER after exhibiting signs of extreme alcohol intoxication.

I'll let him tell the backstory:

I had just started my senior year of high school. My friends and I were planning to attend an all-ages concert in Minneapolis that featured one of our favorite bands.

After school and before leaving for the concert, I guzzled what I thought was a half-bottle of rum, hoping it would give me a "nice buzz" for the evening. It wasn't long before my friends arrived and off we went.

About halfway to the concert venue, it hit me like a ton of bricks. Everything became fuzzy and blurry as I drifted in and out of consciousness. By the time my friends parked the car, they realized I was completely wasted but nonetheless thought they could "contain me."

I don't remember what else happened that night, but later learned that my friends helped drag me to the concert venue, where a slow-moving line of people were waiting to enter. I became agitated by the delay and obnoxiously pushed my way to the front.

The next thing my friends saw was me being thrown airborne (literally) out of the club, onto the concrete sidewalk. Moments later, a bouncer pounced on top of me shouting, "Wanna threaten me again, (expletive)?"

It wasn't long before the police arrived. After giving them a piece of my mind, I was quickly introduced to a flog of nightsticks. Once handcuffed, they transported me to the nearest ER. As if I hadn't already suffered enough indignity, I wet myself in the back of the squad car.

A rational person would have used that experience as an impetus to turn their life around. But not me. I instead wore it as a badge of honor, thinking it had earned me some type of hero status among my peers.

It didn't. After that night, most of them wanted nothing more to do with me.

I don't recall what Chris's blood alcohol content (BAC) was that night, but on subsequent trips to ERs in the years that followed, it generally ranged between .250 and .450. Loss of consciousness typically occurs between .250 and .399, and anything above .400 can trigger a coma—and even death—due to respiratory arrest.

Chris's first night in the ER marked the beginning of my 18-year journey as the father of an alcoholic son. Eighteen years characterized by lies, stolen money, arrests, late-night phone calls from jail, DUIs, ruined family celebrations, public humiliations, extorted threats of suicide, failed rehabs, and more. Each incident evoked anguish, worry, disappointment, and tears—not just by me, but by other family members and friends who, like me, knew Chris best and loved him most.

On some of our trips to ERs, Chris's mother and I witnessed him being restrained on gurneys by doctors and nurses trying to prevent him from lapsing into a coma. Their reward? Listening to Chris spew obscenities at them. The following day became a humbling ritual of bringing flowers and cards to the ER staff, explaining, "This isn't how we raised him." They would thank us for the nice gesture and extend sympathetic nods of understanding. Clearly, Chris wasn't their first, nor last, encounter with a belligerent drunk.

The early years of Chris's addiction became an extended season of confronting my own failure as a Christian parent. *What could I have done differently to prevent this from happening? More father and son "bonding" time? More extracurricular activities at school and church to keep him occupied? More scrutiny of who his friends were and what they were doing together? And why did it take me so painfully long to even acknowledge the seriousness of his addiction?*

A growing sense of guilt and remorse filled my heart, which ultimately led me to seek God's forgiveness for whatever role my permissive and passive parenting played in Chris's addiction.

James, the brother of Jesus, described my condition perfectly: "So whoever knows the right thing to do and fails to do it, for him it is sin" (James 4:17, ESV). Upon receiving God's forgiveness, I was finally able to forgive myself, and refocus my energy on what, if anything, I could do to help my son. But I didn't realize until years later that my "helping" was actually hurting Chris's chances for recovery—and prolonging his addiction.

This journey also taught me that the road to recovery can be long and arduous, replete with many detours and setbacks. I soon learned an entirely new vernacular, which included words like denial, enabling, codependency, powerlessness, accountability, consequences, boundaries, and detachment.

I came from a family where no one had ever struggled with alcohol or drugs (blessedly), so this was new territory for me— a dark, confusing, and frightening territory that was threatening to destroy my son. And I just wanted to fix it and make it disappear. Quickly.

The Growing Up Years

Chris was the firstborn of two loving parents. He was surrounded by an extended family of loving grandmas, grandpas, aunts, uncles, and cousins, most of whom lived in close proximity to one another. His mother and I placed a high priority on nurturing loving, family relationships. Then, at age five, Chris became big brother to a sister, Traci. Our family seemed complete. And for a while, it was.

During Chris's grade school years, he made friends easily and loved playing sports and video games. By all outward appearances, he seemed a pretty normal and happy fellow. But in the classroom, it soon became evident, despite having above average cognitive and verbal abilities, Chris wasn't a traditional classroom learner—a condition that would follow him into middle school where he was diagnosed with Attention Deficit Disorder (ADD).

To compensate for his academic shortcomings, Chris began acting out with disruptive behavior in the third and fourth grades. As a consequence, he frequently lost privileges at school and at home, yet nothing we or his teachers did seemed to improve his behavior.

Our Family Divides

A 1957 issue of Reader's Digest® quoted American writer John Allen Saunders with writing the following: "Life is what happens to us while we are making other plans" (later modified and popularized in John Lennon's 1980 song, "Beautiful Boy (Darling Boy))." (Lennon, 1980)

That's an apt description of my life during this time. I was working in various sales and marketing jobs that required extensive overnight travel and precious time away from family. I justified the sacrifice by convincing myself I was building a better future for all of us. But the strain of frequent absences eventually caused my wife and I to drift apart, culminating with us separating when Chris and Traci were just 11 and five. Sadly, after submitting to individual and joint Christian counseling for more than a year, we divorced after 13 years of marriage.

It's impossible to know how much, if any, our divorce contributed to Chris's later difficulties. But while our kids acclimated to living at both Mom's house and Dad's house, we consistently reinforced to them that our divorce wasn't their fault—it was ours—and that we loved both of them unconditionally. At the risk of sounding cliché, I think we succeeded in creating a "new normal" for our kids that was characterized by many wonderful experiences and happy memories.

Moving On

I remarried several years later, having met my wife-to-be at a Christian singles event. Chris (14) and Traci (8) were introduced to their new stepmother, Nancie, and stepsister, Melinda (11). Things were good though not perfect during those early years, as together we adapted to the normal stresses that blended families commonly experience. Nonetheless, things were mostly harmonious in our newly christened household.

Chris entered middle school and his academic challenges followed him. Fearing his classroom difficulties were becoming a drag on his self-esteem, his mother and I exposed him to various afterschool activities, such as wrestling and basketball, hoping to find something that would spark his interest and help him feel good about himself.

While these actions garnered limited success, the real breakthrough occurred one Saturday morning when Chris was fifteen. I remember us discussing the musical proficiency (or lack thereof) of his favorite rock musicians—most notably,

Kurt Cobain of Nirvana. Being an average guitar player myself, I bragged to Chris that I could teach him to play his favorite Nirvana song in less than an hour, which left him incredulous. Sure enough, within one hour he was playing the song's three chords all by himself—not well, mind you, but well enough to ignite a burning, lifelong passion for playing the guitar.

Music became a rare point of connection between us. Chris couldn't learn the guitar fast enough. Within a year, he had an electric guitar and amplifier, and had formed his own band: "Tugboat." He was ecstatic when they were invited to play at their school's homecoming dance his senior year.

Despite having music and guitars in common, Chris soon began distancing himself from me and the rest of the family. Hanging out with friends, whom I rarely met and knew only by first names (if that), became his primary after-school and weekend activity. He frequently stayed overnight at their houses, but never invited them to ours. And I never called his friends' parents to confirm his story or make sure he was under their parental supervision. I just wanted to avoid the drama of making him angry and the shouting that would ensue.

I eventually learned—much too late—that my passive, conflict-avoiding, "be a friend" approach to parenting would only lead to bigger problems (and greater heartaches) down the road. "Whoever spares the rod hates his son, but he who loves him is diligent to discipline him," (Proverbs 13:24, ESV).

A Downward Spiral

Chris absolutely adored his grandfather (my dad). When he passed away after a long and difficult battle with pancreatic cancer, Chris took it especially hard.

Still in his senior year of high school, Chris found playing in his band a good diversion from confronting his grief. He and his three bandmates would spend most of their free time practicing for upcoming shows at school and parties.

Unbeknownst to me, however, Chris's drinking had become increasingly problematic, especially with his bandmates. They were tired of his alcohol-related antics. So not long after the incident described earlier at the concert venue, they voted to kick him out of the very band he helped to form.

Chris's self-image, which had become fully intertwined with his role in the band, was shattered—compounded further by grief at losing his grandfather and anxiety over his academic deficiencies. He soon began experiencing a loss of hope, and even despaired of life itself.

Chris lost his appetite and dropped 57 pounds over a five-month period before finally leveling off. Having gone from 215 to 158 pounds, he looked almost gaunt on his six-foot, one-inch frame. Doctors couldn't find a physical cause for the weight loss, so we began pursuing psychological ones, which included a myriad of tests and therapy. The results revealed what we already suspected: Chris was clinically depressed over the loss of his grandpa, and the personal trauma of being rejected (betrayed, in his mind) by his closest friends in the band.

Grief ridden, isolated, and stripped of his rock band persona, Chris displayed signs of severe stress and anxiety. He also began hanging out with a new group of older kids, who, like him, seemed devoid of positive meaning and direction in their lives.

Then one night, my phone rang around ten o'clock. The exasperated caller was the proprietor of a pizza restaurant in downtown Minneapolis.

"Your son is passed out drunk in front of my restaurant. Come get him now or I'm calling the cops!"

Thirty-minutes later, after somehow avoiding a speeding ticket, Chris's mother and I arrived at the scene. What we saw caused our hearts to sink.

There was Chris, lying prostrate on the sidewalk, incapable of mumbling anything coherent, his body limp and reeking of alcohol.

After finally getting him to his feet, I began shuffling him to my car while getting an earful from the proprietor: "Your boy's got a real problem. You better get him some help!"

I nodded in tacit agreement, thanking him profusely for not involving the police; although, in retrospect, Chris being sent to a detox center may have served as a much-needed wakeup call—if not for him, then me.

We instead took him to a local ER, where he soon become an all-too-familiar face. Once stabilized, we brought him home to sleep it off.

Six months later, when Chris was eighteen, I received a call at work around ten o'clock one weekday morning. A police officer informed me they had responded to a call from a gas station attendant that a juvenile (Chris) appeared intoxicated when purchasing gas. When they arrived, Chris was still in the car. As soon as he started the engine and drove away, they pulled him over on an exit ramp to a busy freeway.

Upon arriving at the scene, the officer informed me they were placing Chris under arrest for driving under the influence and possession of a half-empty, 1.75-liter bottle of vodka inside the car.

Seeing Chris sitting in the back seat of the police car left me reeling with emotions. Anger. Embarrassment. Hopelessness. And fear—much, much fear. I was afraid something serious was happening that I didn't understand and couldn't control—and I was right.

"Chris, have you been drinking?" I asked rhetorically, speaking through the open rear window.

"No, I haven't had anything to drink," he responded with a distinctly slurred lisp. To no one's surprise, the breathalyzer proved otherwise.

That episode culminated in Chris's first DUI (the first of four over 18 years, which could easily have been many times that number), a revoked license, a trip to rehab, and a fine—which I eventually paid for like any clueless, enabling father would do.

Chris was arrested again just one week later—this time for public drunkenness and repeatedly falling into snowbanks while out walking. The police found a half-empty bottle of vodka in his backpack.

One year down. Seventeen to go.

Is My Story Your Story?

Does my story sound familiar? Do you have a loved one—a child, sibling, parent, work colleague, or close friend—who's struggling with addiction to alcohol or drugs? If so, welcome to The Loved Ones of Addicts Club. This club is exponentially larger than The Addicts Club, because for every one addict there are countless others, like you and me, whose lives are negatively affected by the actions and self-destructive behavior of the addict we love—made only worse by the anguish we feel from taking excessive responsibility for their addiction-related problems. (Congratulations, by the way. You've just learned the meaning of codependence.)

The emotional pain we endure from loving an addict is palpable, and almost impossible to describe to someone who has never walked in our shoes. We worry ourselves sick, with the only antidote being to acquiesce to our loved one's demands (typically money, food, shelter, or transportation). Besides, if we didn't help them, they might stop loving us, right?

But what's the end-result of our *helping*? In the short term, it's resolution of our addict's immediate crisis, which loosens the anxious knot in our stomachs; but long term, it's the perpetuation of their addiction. It's an endless cycle of enabling that only we can stop—if we can just trust God for the strength to do so.

If you love an addict, there are three things you can do—must do—to maintain your sanity while walking through this dark and uncertain valley: 1) Educate yourself on the basics of addiction; 2) equip yourself on managing codependent patterns that lead to paralyzing worry, fear, and despair; and 3) embrace a deeper, closer relationship with God than you ever imagined possible.

Why I Wrote This Book

In writing this book, I'm not suggesting that my story is worse than yours or anyone else's. Far from it. It's just my story—nothing more and nothing less.

My objective was not to write an in-depth, scholarly treatise on codependency. (Frankly, that's way above my pay grade anyway!) Instead, this book is a 21-day devotional. Each devotional chapter contains a practical, easy-to-read lesson (usually with a personal story) on how to positively influence your loved one to a life of sobriety—in addition to things you should avoid doing that can prolong or exacerbate their addiction. I also include biblical inspiration, purposeful prayer, and topic-related questions to reflect on yourself or discuss in a small group.

In effect, this book is a repository of must-have information I wish I had received at the onset of Chris's addiction.

I selected the book's title, *Stop Prolonging Your Loved One's Addiction: How Your 'Helping' May Actually Be Hurting*, based on years of futile effort trying to "cure" Chris of his addiction. Unfortunately, many of my actions only made matters worse. But once I got out of the way and allowed God to perform His redemptive work in my son (mostly in the form of hard consequences), a new course was set into motion, which ultimately led to positive change.

As you may have gleaned from this Introduction (spoiler alert!), Chris is alive and well, having just celebrated six years of sobriety. Praise God!

Perhaps you're reading this book because you're still waiting for God to answer your prayer, and lead your loved one to sobriety. And you're wondering, even doubting, if it will ever happen. I understand. That's how I felt for many years. If this is your present situation, then this book may be God-ordained reading for you.

Throughout these pages, I recount personal stories that invariably paint Chris in an unflattering light. But that was the "old Chris." If you met the new and improved "sober Chris," you'd encounter a profoundly loving, empathetic, and humble young man, whom you'd like to know and have as a friend.

Chris gave me permission to share our stories with you. He did so to "pay it forward" with people experiencing similar hardships with their addicted loved ones. For this selfless gesture, Chris has earned my heartfelt respect and gratitude. He is, in every sense of the word, my hero.

How to Read This Book

If you are experiencing debilitating anxiety over your loved one's addiction, you may want to read this book through in two or three sittings to quickly absorb its contents. Or, if you prefer, read the chapter headings on the Contents page and select one that describes your current situation. Otherwise, I encourage you to read at a comfortable pace—perhaps a chapter a day for 21 days—to allow sufficient time to fully meditate on its substance.

Finally, it's my fervent prayer that hundreds of "Loved Ones of Addicts" support groups will form throughout the country, where like-minded people of faith can gather each week to read from this and other faith-based books, discuss its contents, and share their experiences in a safe and confidential setting. In doing so, they will extend each other love, support, prayer, and encouragement while navigating this difficult journey together—with God's help.

Perhaps God is calling you to form such a group in your church or community. If so, refer to the chapter titled, "Starting a 'Loved Ones of Addicts' Support Group."

May God bless you and your loved one. My prayers are with both of you.

Day 1:

Stop Denying

"The pride of your heart has deceived you ..."
(Obadiah 1:3, NIV).

In judging the Edomites for cursing Israel, God spoke through the prophet Obadiah in identifying the root cause of their sin: their prideful hearts had deceived them.

Similarly, it was pride and self-deception that caused me to deny my 17-year-old son's addiction to alcohol. I refused to believe it.

That's something that happens to other people's kids. It's just a phase he's going through. Besides, I don't have time for such drama. I have a new wife and blended family to care for. My career is on track. And financially, we're feeling pretty secure. Why obsess over a problem that doesn't actually exist?

But exist it did. And I was steeped in denial because I didn't want the reality of Chris's addiction to inconvenience or embarrass me. Could I have been any more self-centered?

Jesus said "... you will know the truth, and the truth will set you free" (John 8:32, NIV). This passage urges us to break free from the bondage of sin—which pride certainly is—by acknowledging the clear and evident truth. Jesus' words should convict any of us who deny, in the face of overwhelming evidence, that their loved one struggles with addiction.

By familiarizing yourself with the warning signs of addiction—both behavioral and physical—you can be alerted to the possibility of a loved one who's struggling with a substance abuse problem.

Warning Signs of Addiction (partial list)

Behavioral Changes:	Physical Changes:
- More easily provoked to becoming angry or aggressive - Decline in work or study habits - Less forthright about activities, whereabouts, purchases, etc. - Borrows or steals from loved ones or employer - Altered eating or sleeping patterns - Unexcused absences from school, work, or social engagements - Uncharacteristic changes in mood and temperament - Displays depression, nervousness, lethargy, low self-esteem, or paranoia - Less passionate about activities previously considered enjoyable	- Eyes appear glassy or red - Profuse sweating or involuntary tremors, occasional bloating - Track marks from needle injections - More talkative and excitable; slurred speech - Exhibits apathy, little to no energy - Changes in facial expression, including pupil size and skin color - Nausea, vomiting, nose bleeds - Changes in walking pattern or gait - Poor hygiene or appearance - Uncommon outbreak of skin irritations (acne, rash, etc.) - Inordinate sweating

Once there's irrefutable evidence that your loved one struggles with an addiction, they, on the other hand, may still be in denial about their own condition. What then?

It simply means they are not yet ready to receive the help they desperately need. Until they acknowledge both the existence of their addiction and how powerless they are to overcome it, they will, in all likelihood, be unsuccessful in any type of treatment program. To be sure, there are exceptions, but this is generally the case.

Step 1 in Alcoholics Anonymous states: "We admitted we were powerless over alcohol—that our lives had become unmanageable." (Alcoholics Anonymous, 1939, 1955, 1976, 2001) But even after Chris acknowledged his problem with alcohol, he spent years deceiving himself into thinking he could control it himself, and be a "social drinker" like his friends—a stage that I refer to as "Partial Denial." He persisted in denying that his life had become unmanageable, and that he was powerless over his addiction.

Perhaps a diagram would better describe this process:

An Addict's Path Out of Denial

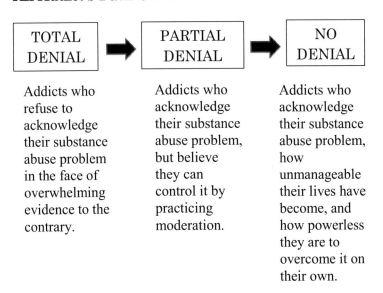

TOTAL DENIAL	PARTIAL DENIAL	NO DENIAL
Addicts who refuse to acknowledge their substance abuse problem in the face of overwhelming evidence to the contrary.	Addicts who acknowledge their substance abuse problem, but believe they can control it by practicing moderation.	Addicts who acknowledge their substance abuse problem, how unmanageable their lives have become, and how powerless they are to overcome it on their own.

So what was the impetus that moved Chris from Total Denial to No Denial? In a word: consequences. Once the consequences of his drinking—including DUIs, trips to ERs, time in jail, loss of friends, broken relationships, fines, and evictions—caused him more pain and hardship than his dread of entering treatment (again), he finally admitted his powerlessness over alcohol and became serious, *truly serious*, about achieving sobriety.

These words may not sound terribly comforting. Trust me, I know. It's anguishing to watch a loved one suffer consequences due to poor choices fueled by their addiction.

Just remember that achieving sobriety rarely happens overnight. It is a process that sometimes includes multiple relapses and trips to treatment. Yet more times than not, it's the self-inflicted consequences that help our loved ones to step out of their denial, acknowledge the existence of their substance problem, and admit how powerless they are to overcome it on their own. Once they achieve this milestone, they are well on their way to experiencing what Jesus promised: "... the truth will set you free" (John 8:32, NIV).

TAKEAWAY:

Learn to recognize the warning signs of addiction. They are good indicators (though not conclusively) that your loved one may have an alcohol or drug addiction. Once an addict acknowledges (1) their addiction exists, (2) their life is unmanageable as a result, and (3) how powerless they are to overcome it on their own, they will be better prepared to enter treatment and achieve lasting sobriety.

GOD'S WORD:

"The Lord is close to the brokenhearted and saves those who are crushed in spirit..." (Psalm 34:18, NIV).

PRAYER:

Lord, we know You care for our loved ones even more than we do, and that it grieves your heart when they make poor choices due to their addiction. Help them, Jesus, to step out of their denial and acknowledge the seriousness of their addiction, even if that requires them to experience hard but necessary consequences.

Amen.

QUESTIONS:

1. Were you ever (or are you now) in denial about your loved one's addiction? Explain.

2. What warning signs of addiction (if any) do you observe in your loved one?

3. Is your loved one in Total Denial, Partial Denial, or No Denial?

4. Describe how you feel when your loved one refuses to acknowledge their addiction or how powerless they are over it? What coping skills, if any, have worked for you?

Day 2:

Stop Enabling

"When he came to his senses, he said, 'How many of my father's hired servants have food to spare, and here I am starving to death'" (Luke 15:17, NIV)!

Are you guilty of doing things for your loved one that they could or should be doing for themselves? If so, you're likely enabling them, and potentially prolonging their addiction. But don't beat yourself up. We do such things because we think we're helping them, and don't realize that we're making matters worse.

Yet as Christ followers, aren't we supposed to display a spirit of servanthood toward one another—especially when it comes to helping our loved ones? Yes, but with an asterisk. First ask yourself this question: Does your loved one need help because they have squandered their own resources to support an alcohol or drug addiction? If so, your "helping" may actually be hurting.

These are the occasions in which tough love must be exhibited with a polite, but firm, "No." The alternative is to enable your loved one and risk worsening their addiction. Enabling shields loved ones from experiencing the consequences of their unhealthy behavior, thus making their pathway to sobriety longer and more arduous.

The need for consequences to transform behavior is wonderfully illustrated in the Parable of the Prodigal Son (Luke 15:11-32). It's about a disobedient son (the younger of two brothers) who demanded that his father pay him his rightful, legal inheritance in advance of his passing.

For a son to make such a request of his living father was highly offensive to Jewish sensibilities. In effect, the son was telling his father, "I wish you were dead." Moreover, for a father to honor such a request, as he does in the Parable, would be viewed as exceedingly generous.

As the story continues, the wayward son, after receiving his early inheritance, "set off for a distant country and there squandered his wealth in wild living" (Luke 15:13, NIV). Desperate for food, he gets a job feeding pigs for money, at which time he has a revelation, as described in Luke 15:17, when " … he came to his senses …" and ultimately returns home to the loving embrace and forgiveness of his father. Clearly, consequences work.

But wait! Didn't the father chase after his son to rescue him from squandering his inheritance and suffering such dire consequences? Nope. The wise and loving father knew that his son's consequences—and all that he would learn from them— would have infinitely greater value than any monetary inheritance. So instead of rescuing his son, the text suggests he waited. Patiently. Prayerfully. Going about his daily business. Fully trusting that one day his son would come to his senses and return home, which is precisely what happened.

The father in this parable refers to God the Father, who joyfully welcomes each of us back into a relationship if we ever fall out of step with Him. Similarly, this is how we must respond toward our loved ones once they "come to their senses." They demonstrate this by acknowledging their addiction exists, their life is out of control, and they lack the willpower necessary to overcome it on their own—underscored by a fervent desire to become sober and drug free.

Upon graduating from high school, Chris attended technical college to study audio recording. He then spent eight years living in Chicago and Santa Monica, trying to establish a foothold for an audio career. But he now concedes there was an ulterior motive for moving away from family and friends: "I purposely wanted to create distance between myself and my loved ones, so they could no longer monitor my worsening alcohol addiction. Once I was free of their constant scrutiny, my addiction had room to flourish."

And flourish it did. During the years when Chris lived in Santa Monica and Chicago (with my enabling, financial assistance, of course), he would regularly run short of money and call me with the same demand: "I need money. They're cutting off my electricity." Or, "My rent is four weeks past due and they're going to evict me." Or, "I haven't eaten in days and need food." You get the idea.

I had little doubt that the circumstances he described were true. But the reason they were true was not for lack of money, but how he chose to spend what money he had. By subsidizing the cost of his groceries, rent, and electricity, I was indirectly enabling him to spend his own money on alcohol, thus perpetuating his addiction. (I warn against doing this repeatedly in this book.)

Deep down, I knew Chris was manipulating me in a game of OPM (i.e., Other People's Money), but I couldn't stomach the thought of him suffering consequences, regardless if they were due to his own poor choices. My enabling behavior continued until I finally met with a Christian therapist, which I describe in a later chapter (Day 14: "Stop Going It Alone").

Loved ones need to be forewarned if you decide to stop doing things for them that they could or should be doing for themselves—that instead of enabling you'll be helping them in more productive ways, such as providing companionship, guidance, encouragement, and empathy. This is necessary so they understand the reason for your change in behavior, and can adjust their expectations accordingly.

Finally, not every enabling situation is black and white. Occasionally there are gray areas with extenuating circumstances. But if you elect to help a loved one do something they could or should be doing for themselves, never do so without first asking God for His direction, and honestly admitting to yourself and one other trusted person the reason for your decision.

TAKEAWAY:

Stop doing things for your loved ones that they could or should be doing for themselves. Your enabling may be shielding them from the consequences of their addiction. Consequences are necessary lessons. When they occur, follow the example of the prodigal son's father: don't give chase to alleviate your loved one's pain; rather, wait for them to "come to their senses."

GOD'S WORD:

"Be on your guard; stand firm in the faith; be courageous; be strong" (1 Corinthians 16:13, NIV).

PRAYER:

Lord, when our loved ones ask for help, help us to correctly discern whether it's something they could or should be doing for themselves.

Amen.

QUESTIONS:

1. What lessons did you learn from the Parable of the Prodigal Son that you hadn't previously considered? What will you do differently?

2. Are you able to stop taking responsibility for your loved one's addiction and instead prayerfully wait for them to "come to their senses," like the prodigal son's father?

3. Do you have difficulty discerning whether your loved one's requests are something they could or should be doing for themselves? How do you decide?

Day 3:

Stop Negotiating

"It is one's honor to avoid strife,
but every fool is quick to quarrel"
(Proverbs 20:3, NIV).

Addicts have a highly developed sense of entitlement. So when they're deprived of things they need or want, they frequently expect their friends and family members to provide it for them.

But as we discussed in the previous chapter, doing things for our loved ones that they could or should be doing for themselves is called enabling, which only serves to prolong their addiction by shielding them from further consequences.

In this chapter, we address the inevitable negotiating (and too often, arguing) that ensues once you say "No" to your loved one's requests or demands.

My best counsel is this: do not open the door to endless negotiating with your loved one. Once you do, your loved one will slice and dice your "unreasonable" position with the deft cross-examining skills of a veteran defense attorney. By the second or third time you say "No," emotions are wearing thin and voices begin rising. Soon you're embroiled in an escalating argument worthy of a reality TV show. Sound familiar?

Among the many things Chris's mother and I endlessly negotiated with Chris were his cellphone and usage fees. "I don't have any credit. No one will sell me a phone," he would tell us. Of course, when I suggested he buy a prepaid phone, that was rejected outright because it "didn't have enough features."

So he felt it was our responsibility to purchase him a phone and add him to our mobile phone plan, with the promise he would reimburse us for his share of the monthly bill. "I can't get a job without a phone," he would say. Or, "You'll never hear from me if I don't have a phone."

So we foolishly acquiesced. Partly from fear of making him angry, and partly from fear of losing all contact with him. He knew the latter was our soft spot, and he exploited it masterfully.

It wasn't long before the excuses began: "I have to pay rent this week and don't have money for my phone." Or, "I don't have money for food; how can I pay for my phone?" It's not that Chris didn't have money to pay for his phone; rather, he didn't have money for his phone after spending what money he had on alcohol.

Although we had peace of mind knowing we could call him at any time (albeit with no assurance he would ever answer), we were, in effect, providing him a privilege he should have been denied as a consequence of his poor choices. Instead, we negotiated, enabled, and ultimately robbed him of a valuable learning opportunity on how to take responsibility for himself.

Much negotiating with addicts is barter-based—meaning you give them what they want now in return for their promise to stop drinking or using drugs. In most cases, they earnestly believe they will follow through on their commitment. Typically, however, they lack the self-control necessary to make good on their promise. It's not that they're deliberately deceptive; it's just the nature of their disease.

Here are some examples of barter-based negotiating:

- "If I can crash at your place, I promise I'll stop drinking."

- "Let me borrow your car while mine is impounded. Not being able to drive is making me anxious and triggering me to use."

- "My sober friends are going out to eat and I don't have any money. Can you borrow me twenty bucks? Otherwise, I'll just hang out with some unsafe friends."

- "If you pay my bail, I'll enter treatment in 30 days."

- "You need to let me leave treatment now! If I ever relapse, I promise I'll come straight back."

- "If you buy me an Xbox, it will keep me occupied so I won't think about using drugs as much."

Most of these statements can be translated this way: "If you don't give me what I want now, I might relapse or worse, and it will all be your fault." Don't fall for it. Be firm, resolute, and decisive in denying their requests. If it's something you're uncertain about, explain that you need time to consider it. If that doesn't suffice, reply in a calm and measured voice: "If you need a decision this moment, my answer is no. If you can give me some time to more fully consider my answer, there's a possibility—but no guarantee. I'm not going to debate this any further."

(A couple tips: Avoid letting your voice become louder when disagreeing with your loved one. It will help keep you in control of the conversation, and your "no" will be viewed as decisive and final, and not open to further negotiation. Also, avoid using words like "always" and "never" in describing your loved one's behavior. Example: "You never follow through on your promises and always leave me feeling disappointed." Such words only serve to shame.)

By consistently and decisively declining a loved one's barter-based requests, they'll be discouraged from making similar ones in the future. And on the occasions they do, they'll be more inclined to accept your initial rejection without entering into prolonged negotiations.

If saying "No" to your loved one is something you've previously tried but later acquiesced to, you'll need the prayerful support of others—such as friends, family, support group partners, a counselor, or pastor—to help you remain strong and follow through.

Finally, sometimes we are the ones—not our loved ones—who initiate the negotiating, thinking we can barter our loved one's promise of sobriety in exchange for giving them something they want. Even worse, I've heard of people who freely supply their loved ones with alcohol and drugs, stipulating they only be consumed under their watchful supervision. By doing so, they rationalize they can monitor their loved one's substance usage and request medical attention if ever needed. Needless to say, such deal making is equally futile and ill-conceived.

TAKEAWAY:

Refrain from endlessly negotiating your loved one's requests (or demands) for things they could or should be providing for themselves—that is, if they weren't already squandering their own resources to support their addiction. Let your "no" mean NO—then allow your loved one to experience the consequences.

GOD'S WORD:

"The heart is deceitful above all things, and desperately sick; who can understand it" (Jeremiah 17:9, ESV)?

PRAYER:

Lord, grant us courage and patience the next time we answer "No" to our loved ones' requests for things they could or should be doing for themselves.

Amen.

QUESTIONS:

1. Do you feel your loved one has "a highly developed sense of entitlement"? If so, why?

2. Can you share an example of a barter-based request your loved one made that was tied to sobriety? How did you respond to it? Would you handle it differently now?

3. Do rejections of your loved one's barter-based requests ever escalate into arguments? What can you do to diffuse the situation next time?

4. Do you have a support system in place for when you make difficult decisions concerning your loved one?

Day 4:

Stop Dithering

"If any of you lacks wisdom, you should ask God, who gives generously to all without finding fault, and it will be given to you" (James 1:5, NIV).

The third chapter of Daniel recounts the story of Shadrach, Meshach, and Abednego—three Jewish men who defied a command from King Nebuchadnezzar (then King of Babylon) that all people should worship his gods and bow down to his golden statue. As punishment for their disobedience, the three men were thrown into a blazing furnace, but not before telling King Nebuchadnezzar, "... the God we serve is able to deliver us from it, and he will deliver us from Your Majesty's hand" (Daniel 3:17, NIV).

Which is precisely what God did. Why? Because Shadrach, Meshach, and Abednego were obedient and faithful to the one true God, the God of Abraham, and did the right thing— something I failed to do on many occasions, but particularly on one lazy, fall Sunday afternoon.

After watching two NFL games on TV, I decided to visit my local Best Buy store. Stepping out of the car, I looked across the crowded parking lot and recognized my late-father's Crown Victoria—the one we allowed Chris to drive while attending vocational college.

Seeing that Chris was sitting alone in the parked car, I decided to investigate further. When I came within 10 yards of the car—despite all the windows being rolled up—I could hear the thumping sound of bass guitar and other instruments playing at deafening levels through the audio speakers.

Chris seemed oblivious to my approach until I stood outside his door. The moment he looked up, I knew there was trouble. His blank expression and glassy eyes gave evidence he was inebriated.

Any lingering doubts he'd been drinking were quickly dispelled once he lowered his window. The pungent smell of alcohol was stifling, emanating not only from Chris's breath but oozing from his pores.

I quickly scanned the car's interior for any sign of beer cans or liquor bottles, but saw nothing. I rhetorically asked him if he'd been drinking—not that I had any doubt, but to give myself time to plan my next move.

Before he began voicing his denial, I lunged inside the open window attempting to remove his keys from the ignition. Anticipating my action, Chris blocked my extended arm with his right hand while rolling up the window with his left, thus forcing my arm into an awkward and dangerous angle.

Seeing that Chris's car was blocked by other parked cars on both sides and the rear, I quickly withdrew my arm and ran to the front of the car, hoping to block his exit. But Chris, who by then was in full panic mode and screaming hysterically, began moving the car forward—slowly, at first, but just enough to let me know he wasn't going to lose this test of wills ... no matter what.

When I finally relented and stepped aside, Chris floored the accelerator and tore off through the congested parking lot at dangerously high speeds with tires screeching.

Within moments, he was gone.

For a moment, I stood there. Stunned by what just happened. The smell of burned rubber still penetrated my nostrils. I quickly called Nancie and described what had happened. When I asked, "What should I do?" I already knew the answer. Nancie, who rarely gets upset or excited, sternly replied, "Call 911! He could have an accident that kills himself or somebody else!"

That's not what I wanted to hear. As the aggrieved father, I instead wanted sympathy. I wanted empathy. But all I got was a dose of common sense. Unlike Shadrach, Meshach, and Abednego, I deliberately chose not to do the right thing—even after being admonished to do so by my wife.

Instead of being horrified at the prospect of Chris driving drunk and potentially hurting himself or someone else, I was more worried he'd be arrested and go to jail, be convicted of another DUI, lose his license, incur more fines (which I would foolishly pay), be placed on probation, get kicked out of school, and, what I feared most, become angry with me.

By the grace of God, no one was hurt that Sunday afternoon, and Chris arrived home safely. But it could just as easily have ended in tragedy, and me living each day of the rest of my life wondering if I could have prevented it—if I had only done the right thing.

Moreover, the consequences I sought to protect Chris from could very well have expedited his recovery. Instead, I quite possibly—even probably—prolonged his addiction by trying to protect him from the consequences of his actions.

But did I learn my lesson? I thought I had ... until a similar situation occurred several years later. More on that in the next chapter ("Day 5: Stop Obsessing").

As James 1:15 promises, if we ever need wisdom, just ask God and He will provide it. But then it's up to us, as obedient followers of Christ, to act on that wisdom and do the right thing.

TAKEAWAY:

Have the courage to make difficult decisions if your loved one becomes a threat to themselves and/or others, such as contacting the police if they are driving impaired. Such decisions may result in extremely harsh consequences, which may lead them to receive much-needed treatment. Your action may prevent a tragic outcome for themselves or someone else.

GOD'S WORD:

"Whoever walks in integrity walks securely, but whoever takes crooked paths will be found out" (Proverbs 10:9, NIV).

PRAYER:

Lord, grant us wisdom and courage to do the right thing when making hard decisions that affect our loved ones.

Amen.

QUESTIONS:

1. Can you recall a situation when you needed to make a hard decision concerning your loved one's addiction— a decision that they disagreed with? Did you base any part of your decision on whether it would cause conflict?

2. If faced with the same situation Jon described in this chapter, would you report your loved one to the police? Why or why not?

3. What's the best way of discerning whether the action you need to take is consistent with godly wisdom?

Day 5:

Stop Obsessing

*"You say ... 'I have the right to do anything,'— but I will not
be mastered by anything" (1 Corinthians 6:12, NIV).*

S ome Corinthian Christians thought they could engage in
deviant behavior since they were "in Christ," and thus
protected by God's grace. The expression, "I have the
right to do anything" (1 Corinthians 10:23, NIV) became a
popular slogan that expressed this sentiment.

But the Apostle Paul tried to correct this "free grace"
thinking by admonishing them that "[we] will not be mastered
by anything" (1 Corinthians 6:12, above). The meaning has
clear implications for our loved ones, and for us as well.

Whereas Chris was mastered by an addiction to alcohol, I
was mastered by an obsessive need to know where Chris was
and what he was doing—at all times. Was he drinking? Was he
in danger? I had to know.

My obsession manifested itself in various ways: sending
him endless texts and emails; monitoring his social media;
driving by his apartment, workplace, or friends' houses looking
for his car; calling his sister and mother to ask if they had seen
or heard from him; and so on. I became so overwrought with
worry at the prospect of him drinking that my only relief was
to find evidence that he wasn't.

Having moderated many Loved Ones of Addicts support
groups, I know this is a common and debilitating behavior.
Precious time that could otherwise be spent pursuing useful

endeavors—growing in the Lord, serving the needy, making new relationships—is squandered trying to make our fear of the unknown disappear.

Eventually, these futile surveilling tactics only serve to agitate our loved ones, driving them even further away from us. They resent the scrutiny of being spied upon as if they were children, which itself could trigger an onset of substance use.

Does this mean you should never reach out to your loved one? Of course not! But do so just as you would if their addiction didn't exist. Have conversations about things you would normally talk about—food, sports, current events, work, etc. And don't probe for an admission about their substance use. In short, act as though you have a normal relationship— even though there's an elephant in the room.

So how do we avoid obsessing (or being mastered, as Paul put it) about our loved ones' welfare? For many of us, the root cause of our obsessing stems from not being focused on God and trusting in His Divine Providence. Whenever that happens, we risk succumbing to fear and worry, leading to an obsessive need for our own selves—not God—to be in control.

I remember leaving church one cold and snowy evening when my phone rang. It was Chris. Fearing the worst, my heart began racing and the all-too-familiar knot in my stomach grew tighter.

"Chris, what's up?" I asked hesitantly.

In slurred speech that confirmed my suspicion, he said: "I just got to work and no one's here except people I don't know. They're looking at me funny. And why is it so dark outside?"

He was disoriented from a combination of alcohol and prescription drugs, and had confused nighttime with morning.

And those people he was seeing? They were the evening cleaning crew.

"Sit tight and I'll come give you a ride home," I said, hoping to dissuade him from driving and potentially hurting himself and others. But he abruptly hung up and ignored my subsequent calls and text messages.

Feeling panicked and consumed by fear, I completely forgot the lesson I learned several years earlier in the Best Buy parking lot (see "Day 4: Stop Dithering"). Instead of taking deep breaths, alerting the police, and praying for God's protection over everyone involved, I spent two hours obsessing about Chris's whereabouts and physical wellbeing.

I eventually made the long drive to his apartment and found his car parked outside his building. By the grace of God, he had made it home safely. This time, anyway. But how would I have felt, or lived with myself for the rest of my life, if he or others had been hurt or even killed when I could have done something to potentially prevent it?

Once again, I allowed my emotions to dictate my actions, and failed to do the right thing. "The Lord is more pleased when we do what is right and just than when we offer him sacrifices" (Proverbs 21:3, NLT).

Of course, had I alerted the police that night, Chris might have been arrested for another DUI. But that happened anyway a year or so later, which led to him getting some much-needed treatment. Yet again, my habitual obsessing and "protecting" only clouded my better judgment.

Embrace this reality: We are as powerless over our loved ones' actions as our loved ones are over their own addictions. And our lives can become equally as unmanageable as theirs by constantly obsessing over their welfare.

There's a frequently repeated slogan in addiction groups that's equally relevant for us: "Let go and let God!"

TAKEAWAY:

Stop obsessively trying to monitor the whereabouts and activities of your loved one. Continual stalking via phone calls, text messaging, social media, and drive-bys will only serve to agitate them and create discord in your relationship. Focus instead on praying for their protection and sobriety.

GOD'S WORD:

"...for God gave us a spirit not of fear but of power and love and self-control" (2 Timothy 1:7, ESV).

PRAYER:

Lord, when we obsess over not knowing if our loved ones are safe or what they are doing, calm us with your abiding peace that surpasses all understanding. Help us to fully trust in your sovereign protection.

Amen.

QUESTIONS:

1. Do you obsessively worry that your loved one is drinking? Using drugs? What do you do to remedy it?

2. Has your loved one ever expressed annoyance at your continual monitoring of their actions?

3. Can you learn to "let go and let God" and not be mastered by obsessive behavior? What will you do differently?

Day 6:

Stop Bailing

"Do not be deceived: God cannot be mocked.
A man reaps what he sows" (Galatians 6:7, NIV).

The first time Chris was incarcerated, he was in Cook County Jail in Chicago—one of the most notorious jails in the country. To no one's surprise, it was for an alcohol-related offense.

Chris was desperate, describing conditions so deplorable I feared for his safety. With my stomach in knots, I immediately contacted a bail bondsman to "rescue" him from jail—ASAP.

Within hours, Chris was released and back home ... and, thanks to me, happily resuming his ever-worsening alcohol addiction. Which made me wonder: *Why did I have such a panic-stricken reaction to him being in jail? Was it because he sounded so afraid and remorseful on the phone, and that he gave every assurance this would never happen again?*

But it did happen again. Then again and again. And there I was each time, with a handful of cash to make the problem "go away."

Years later I had an appointment with a Christian therapist just after Chris had been sent to jail. When I shared the distressing news, he responded with an enthusiastic, "That's great!"

"But," I replied, "he might lose his job and his apartment if he doesn't get out!"

"Even better!" he said—this time a tad too gleefully. I found his lack of empathy profoundly annoying.

But I eventually came to understand the important point he was making: When addicts lose their freedom by being confined in a cramped jail cell, they sometimes gain a perspective on life they might otherwise never see. An epiphany, of sorts.

Inside the lonely confines of a jail cell, during rare moments of God-ordained self-reflection and introspection, addicts can confront their inner demons by asking questions like: *"Why am I destroying my life?";* *"Why do I keep hurting the people who love me most?";* *"How can I cure my addiction?";* and *"Does God have a plan for my life?"*

For such addicts, jail can become their own Damascus Road experience—a complete bottoming out, so to speak, and they miraculously never use alcohol or drugs again. Sadly, this is not the case with most addicts, nor was it the case with Chris.

Nonetheless, even if a jail cell experience doesn't lead to instant sobriety, it frequently yields positive results in the form of addicts acknowledging—perhaps for the first time—how powerless they are to alcohol or drugs (i.e., Step 1 of The 12 Steps), and commit themselves to entering rehab or pursuing some other form of recovery treatment.

My point is this: If your loved one is in jail due to substance abuse, follow the scriptural example of the prodigal son's father (see Luke 15:11-32): Don't send a rescue mission! Instead, consider the benefits of allowing your loved one to come to their senses by letting things take their natural course.

During this time, some practical advice might include:

1. Reading and memorizing Scripture to reduce your anxiety (such as Philippians 4)

2. Praying for God's strength, peace, and wisdom

3. Reciting the Serenity Prayer

4. Asking your support group friends to come alongside you for comfort and strength

Ask yourself the following question: Is there more to be gained by jail or bail?

If you choose the latter, I respect your decision and won't judge you for making it. Those who say it's always best to leave a loved one in jail to "learn their lesson" have typically, by the grace of God, never had to make such a decision themselves. Were it only so easy for the rest of us.

That being said, think long and hard before denying your loved one the introspection that comes from a jail cell experience. Equally important, by helping your loved one to avoid the consequences of being incarcerated—which may include loss of income, independence, living arrangements, transportation, relationships, and more—you may unwittingly be perpetuating their addiction. Jail may be the tough love that they desperately need.

Making such a decision is never easy. So don't decide it alone. Draw close to God by praying for His guidance. Then seek advice from a trusted family or support group member, pastor, or counselor.

TAKEAWAY:

Bailing a loved one out of jail may deny them the forced introspection that often comes from being incarcerated— including an honest self-assessment of their own addiction, and the negative repercussions it's had on themselves and others. Such reflection may even lead them to enter treatment. Pray for God's guidance; then seek the counsel of a trusted friend or advisor before making your decision.

GOD'S WORD:

"So do not fear, for I am with you; do not be dismayed, for I am your God. I will strengthen you and help you; I will uphold you with my righteous right hand" (Isaiah 41:10, NIV).

PRAYER:

Lord, should our loved ones ever become incarcerated, grant us peace and wisdom in deciding how best to help them— especially as it pertains to arranging them bail.

Amen.

QUESTIONS:

1. Describe the emotions you would feel if your loved one called to say they were in jail due to their substance abuse, and they needed you to bail them out?

2. How can you prepare for your loved one's angry reaction if you choose not to bail them out? Are you afraid they could become violent upon their release?

3. Should you tell your loved one in advance that you will not bail them out if they ever go to jail?

Day 7:

Stop Provoking

"The soothing tongue is a tree of life,
but a perverse tongue crushes the spirit"
(Proverbs 15:4, NIV).

Have you ever said something you thought was perfectly innocent, only later to learn that your words had offended someone? This can easily occur when speaking with an addict. A word or phrase you deem perfectly benign can unwittingly crush their spirit (ref. Proverbs 15:4 above).

I said such things routinely to Chris. My purpose was to help him see how desperately I wanted him to be sober. In reality, saying them made me feel better, but only alienated Chris. He found them offensive because they were things he already knew, and didn't need me to keep reminding him.

But I repeated them anyway because I was afraid he'd forget. Or that repeating them would somehow underscore their importance and make a bigger impression on him. Sadly, I was only crushing his spirit.

Here are some examples:

1. When Chris went out with friends, I would invariably ask: "Are they 'safe friends'?"

2. Or when saying goodbye, I would always add, "Be good!" This was my code for "Don't drink!"

3. Or proclaiming the number of days he'd been sober. "Ten days!" Or "Twenty days!" (This became an especially obnoxious practice after Chris had completed a rehab.)

You may read these "good-hearted" statements and think, *What's the big deal? Aren't these just reminders to do the right thing and make good choices?*

Technically, yes. But from Chris's perspective, they placed inordinate pressure on him not to screw up and disappoint everyone (again). And the prospect of disappointing a loved one can be profoundly upsetting to an addict, and can itself trigger a relapse.

Ultimately, Chris became sober once he was ready—not out of deference to me or anyone else. My annoying reminders to avoid "unsafe people" and "be good" had no positive effect, and only added to his fear of disappointing his loved ones. Neither did my constant scorecard announcements of his successive sober days. When Chris finally became serious about getting sober, *he* was the one proclaiming his number of sober days—not me—which was far more meaningful.

If you have something to say to your loved one about their addiction (assuming they even acknowledge it exists), do so by having a real conversation, not by cloaking your sentiments in rhetorical phrases and euphemisms.

But exercise caution. Talking to an addict about their addiction can create a highly charged atmosphere, which is why such conversations should have parameters and structure. Let me explain.

For a number of years, whenever Chris and I got together, I would talk incessantly about his addiction and recovery issues, and practically nothing else. It was exhausting—not only for him, but me as well.

And so, at the advice of my counselor, Chris and I mutually agreed to schedule 10 minutes each week when I could ask him any questions (within reason) about his addiction and recovery progress, and he, in return, would be completely forthright in his answers.

Perhaps for you and your loved one, the frequency and duration of such a conversation would be different, but it needs to be mutually agreeable.

When Chris and I finished our 10-minute Q&A each week, I felt like the air had been cleared (at least for a while), and we could enjoy some semblance of a normal relationship, like talking about sports, current events, seeing a movie together, or just enjoying one another's company in silence.

My point is this: Those 10 minutes helped significantly reduce my need to obsess and worry about Chris.

However, your mutual sit-downs will serve no purpose—other than to make matters worse—if they degenerate into anger and shouting. Endeavor instead to remain calm and control your emotions. Venting might feel good in the moment, but the collateral damage to your relationship can be long-lasting and leave deep scars that are difficult to heal.

As I share in other chapters, I harbored deep anger and resentment toward Chris for many years. I hated how his addiction had intruded on my life, and how my frustration would manifest itself toward him (and others) at the slightest provocation. My disgust was not only evident in my verbal communication, but in my texts, emails, and nonverbal language as well.

Once I accepted that Chris's sobriety was his responsibility, not mine, I was better able to detach from the present situation and maintain my composure when in his presence.

Nonetheless, there still were times, when Chris and I would discuss his disappointing recovery progress, that I would feel my blood pressure rise and impatience taking over. But I learned to practice an effective technique that helped prevent our conversations from escalating into arguments.

How to Prevent Tough Conversations from Turning Into Arguments

1. Consciously filter and re-filter your words before allowing them to leave your mouth. "...it is not what goes into the mouth that defiles a person, but what comes out of the mouth" (Matthew 15:11, ESV).

2. Deliberately control the pitch and volume of your voice, so that it always projects a caring and conversational tone. "A soft answer turns away wrath, but a harsh word stirs up anger" (Proverbs 15:1, ESV).

3. Empathetically listen much more than you speak. "The one who has knowledge uses words with restraint" (Proverbs 17:27, NIV).

It's amazing how many arguments can be abated by simply following these three rules, which are solidly grounded in Scripture. I pray they will help promote safe conversations between you and your loved one, and protect and preserve your relationship.

TAKEAWAY:

Avoid constantly reminding your loved one not to use alcohol or drugs. They already know. Your tedious "suggestions" will only place inordinate pressure on them not to screw up and disappoint their loved ones (again). Instead, schedule a regular time for having calm, candid conversations about their sobriety progress.

GOD'S WORD:

"Let your conversation be always full of grace, seasoned with salt, so that you may know how to answer everyone" (Colossians 4:6, NIV).

PRAYER:

Lord, help us to guard our tongues to avoid offending our loved ones. And help us to be empathetic listeners when our loved ones confide with us about their addiction struggles.

Amen.

QUESTIONS:

1. Are there things you say to your loved one that could be crushing their spirit? Give an example.

2. When talking with your loved one, do you discuss their addiction and recovery progress to the point they become provoked? If so, would it make sense to schedule a specific time and time limit for such conversations?

3. Would practicing "How to Prevent Tough Conversations from Turning Into Arguments" be beneficial when talking

with your loved one? Share an instance when it would have helped.

Day 8:

Stop Confronting—
Start Understanding

"In your anger do not sin: Do not let the sun go down while
you are still angry, and do not give the devil a foothold"
(Ephesians 4:26-27, NIV).

I have yet to meet a loved one of an addict who has never become angry at their addict's repeated substance abuse and poor choices. If you're the exception, I applaud your self-restraint. But becoming angry isn't necessarily a sin (even Jesus became angry); rather, it's how we process and manifest our anger that determines whether it's appropriate.

An incident involving Chris at my mother's visitation service illustrates my point.

Permit me to describe my mom in as few words as possible: She loved Jesus; she loved her family; and she loved everyone else—in that order.

She loved celebrating other people's successes. When others suffered hardship or disappointments, she suffered right alongside them with genuine care and empathy. Which is why it was so heartbreaking when she—of all people—began to display signs of dementia.

After five years of gradual decline, she struggled to even remember her children's names and faces. Yet in spite of her illness, she still had rare but precious moments of clarity when she spoke lovingly about Jesus, and her yearning to be with Him in Heaven.

On the morning the Lord called her home, I held her weak and frail body in my arms during her final 30-minutes of life. In between my tearful recitations of Psalm 23, I whispered, "Go home to Jesus, Mom ... go home to Jesus. He's waiting for you. We love you—and we'll see you again soon." Then she was gone—having drifted from my arms into the outstretched arms of her Savior.

We arranged a visitation service the evening before her funeral. It was both comforting and cathartic to hear friends and family share stories of her many acts of kindness.

Then Chris arrived.

It was obvious to me he had been drinking. Not to the point of inebriation, but enough to cause me and others anxiety and embarrassment.

How could he disrespect his grandmother—and me—like this? Couldn't he set aside drinking for just one day?

I later learned Chris had spent most the day creating a beautiful video montage of my mother's life, which we played at both her visitation service that night and her funeral the next day. Chris loved his grandmother deeply, and the process of creating the video triggered an onslaught of sadness and grief, from which he sought relief the only way he knew how.

Nonetheless, I was indignant, and came perilously close to confronting Chris in the presence of family and friends. My daughter, Traci, sensing my growing anger, wisely kept the two of us apart, allowing me time to regain my composure. Having avoided creating a spectacle, my mother's visitation service proceeded without incident; yet my anger raged on.

The visitation service caused me to recall a similar incident several years earlier. Chris agreed to attend Christmas Eve services with me, my wife Nancie (Chris's stepmom), and his grandma. It was a big deal for him to join us, since it was held at the church where I was employed at the time.

Chris was dropped off at the church by a friend. When he came through the door, we welcomed him warmly and headed for the elevator.

The elevator was crowded, but there was just enough room for the four of us. Once inside, however, it hit me—the smell of alcohol emanating from Chris was unmistakable. I could feel my heartrate and blood pressure begin to rise. Not today! Not here! Not in front of my friends and coworkers!

I became awash with feelings of embarrassment and humiliation—especially when another gentleman on the elevator began looking at Chris suspiciously. I began thinking, *Do I just take him to my car and wait for Nancie and mom to join us after the service?*

I quickly prayed for God's direction—and what immediately entered my mind was one question: Isn't this precisely where he should be?

I felt convicted. Why remove Chris and preclude the possibility of God performing a miracle in his life, or perhaps planting a seed that might blossom into sobriety somewhere down the road?

To be sure, had Chris been stumbling and incoherent, I would have been forced to remove him. But he seemed sufficiently alert and responsive that I opted not to rock the boat. Despite the fact that he slept through much of the service, I nonetheless was glad that I didn't risk making a scene. It allowed us to return home afterward and enjoy a wonderful Christmas Eve dinner and family celebration.

The lesson I learned that Christmas Eve, and was later reminded of after my mother's visitation service, was that confronting Chris only to vent anger—especially when he was intoxicated—might make me feel better in the moment but could damage our relationship beyond repair.

Chris was, after all, an alcoholic. It should come as no surprise when he displayed signs of drinking. As long as he was not a present danger to himself or others, I found it best—in lieu of confronting him each time he smelled of alcohol—to leave well enough alone and behave as normally as possible toward him.

This approach seemed more God-honoring and protective of our relationship. So the next time I saw Chris sober, I could calmly, yet firmly—without emotion or condemnation—privately tell him I knew he had been drinking on a previous occasion, and share how it made me feel.

In virtually every instance, it is counterproductive to try reasoning with, or confronting someone who is under the influence of an addictive substance. Avoiding such volatile encounters will help keep the lines of future conversations open, without risking long-term or permanent damage to your relationship.

Let's embrace the words of Jesus' brother, James: "Everyone should be quick to listen, slow to speak and slow to become angry" (James 1:19, NIV).

TAKEAWAY:

Avoid projecting anger toward your loved one—especially when they are impaired by an addictive substance. Such confrontation is almost never productive. More probably, it could damage your relationship beyond repair. Choose instead to project Christ-like love and compassion.

GOD'S WORD:

"Refrain from anger and turn from wrath; do not fret—it leads only to evil" (Psalm 37:8, NIV).

PRAYER:

Heavenly Father, if we ever feel humiliated by our loved ones' addictions, remind us of the greater humiliation you endured, on the cross, for the forgiveness of our sins.

Amen.

QUESTIONS:

1. Has your loved one ever embarrassed or humiliated you while under the influence of alcohol or drugs? If yes, briefly share your story and how you felt and reacted afterward.

2. Do you agree that it's counterproductive to confront your loved one each time they appear moderately under the influence of an addictive substance? Do you think it's better to calmly discuss it with them later when they are sober?

3. How much of your anger is rooted in worrying what other people might think of you due to the actions of your loved one?

Day 9:

Stop Raging—Start Detaching

"Do not be quickly provoked in your spirit,
for anger resides in the lap of fools"
(Ecclesiastes 7:9, NIV).

I once attended a Christian conference I had eagerly been looking forward to. Unfortunately, the conference included an evening session that conflicted with a local NBA game for which I had two free tickets. As much as I wanted to attend the conference, I thought the game would provide a good opportunity for Chris and me to have some fun together, and to enjoy a respite from the constant focus on his addiction.

Certainly, I thought, Chris would conduct himself appropriately during the day and be sober for the game that night. But the moment he stepped into my car for our ride to the arena, the smell of his breath and his altered speech gave evidence to the contrary. He wasn't "fall down drunk," but slightly impaired, nonetheless. I was so angry. I wanted to shout, "Don't you know what I gave up to be with you tonight? Forget the game! Get out of my car and go sober up!"

But I didn't.

By the time we arrived at the parking lot, the obvious tension could be cut with a knife. Chris said, "If you want to just take me home and not go to the game, that's fine."

So I had a choice to make. Do I take him back home to demonstrate how angry I was and teach him a lesson (and, in the process, miss both the game and the conference)? Or do I view the situation through an entirely different lens—a lens that viewed Chris's addiction as being his problem and responsibility to overcome, not my own—and to grant myself permission to enjoy the evening with him, despite the circumstances?

I chose the latter … and I'm glad I did. Despite Chris being slightly impaired, we nonetheless enjoyed a wonderful evening together and had great conversations that I remember to this day. Before he got out of my car when I brought him home, I said, "Chris, this was a lot of fun! I could tell you'd been drinking earlier today, but I also want you to know that I love you, and that I truly believe, with God's help, you can become sober and turn your life around."

I couldn't be sure, but in the darkness of night I believe I saw tears welling up in Chris's eyes, and he said, "I love you too, Dad. Thanks for taking me to the game. It was fun."

This was clearly a more positive outcome than if I had skipped the game and taken him back home in a fit of rage.

That being said, some may argue that I was overly permissive and missed a great opportunity to exert tough love. I understand why they might think that way. So allow me to elaborate more fully on what led to my decision.

The principle I practiced that night is called detachment. Detachment is based on the belief that each person is ultimately responsible for their own problems—a mindset that's consistent with the Apostle Paul's assertion in Galatians 6:5: "For each will have to bear his own load" (NIV).

Detachment doesn't mean you've stopped loving your loved one or no longer care about their addiction. Nor does it mean you've become indifferent to how their poor choices have negatively affected your own life.

Detachment is a process by which we separate ourselves from taking responsibility for our loved one's issues. More specifically, it's a mental, emotional, and—if circumstances warrant—physical separation from our loved one's addiction-related problems, which cause us inordinate worry and anguish. Detachment can only occur when we acknowledge, perhaps for the first time, that we can neither cure our loved one's addiction nor solve their problems for them. Only they can do that—once they've decided to make doing so their highest priority.

I would physically detach from Chris only when feeling so overwrought by his addiction issues that I just needed to escape from the drama. Sometimes it was just going to a movie or eating out with my wife in peace. Other times I would need several days to unwind. As a precaution, each time I went into physical detachment mode, I informed Chris and one or more of my family members that I was turning off my cellphone and going "off the grid." These needed respites afforded me the opportunity to fully decompress, forget about Chris's issues, and re-center my mind, body, and spirit.

Al-Anon describes detachment this way:

"... detachment means to separate ourselves emotionally and spiritually from other people. If someone we love had the flu and cancelled plans with us, most of us would understand ... When alcoholism causes a change in plans, or sends harsh words or other unacceptable behavior in our direction, we needn't take it any more personally than we would take the flu symptoms. It is the disease rather than the individual that is responsible." (How Al-Anon Works for Families and Friends of Alcoholics)

Remember, you can still "love the person without loving the behavior" (author unknown). By doing so, you humbly step back, pray for your loved one's protection and sobriety, and recognize that their addiction is their battle to win—not yours. Then patiently wait for them to step out of their denial, acknowledge how powerless they are to solve their addiction on their own (no doubt after many consequences), and embrace sobriety.

TAKEAWAY:

Don't assume responsibility for your loved one's addiction-related issues. Only they can resolve them. Learn to detach yourself mentally, emotionally, and even physically, when needed, from the stress and drama of their problems. Refrain from personalizing any inappropriate behavior they may direct toward you. Remember, you can "love the person without loving the behavior."

GOD'S WORD:

"The Lord is my strength and my shield; my heart trusts in him, and he helps me" (Psalm 28:7, NIV).

PRAYER:

Lord, help us to love our addicts without loving their behavior, and to detach from their self-destructive choices in healthy ways. When we despair, remind us that our loved ones' problems are their responsibility to correct, not ours.

Amen.

QUESTIONS:

1. How would you react if your loved one agreed to meet you for an event, and then arrived displaying signs of being under the influence? Would you handle it any differently after reading this chapter?

2. Do you sometimes feel responsible for your loved one's addiction? If so, are you capable of detaching yourself from their problems and releasing yourself of this burden?

3. By "loving the person without loving the behavior," do you think you can detach more effectively when your loved one makes poor choices? If not, why not?

Day 10:

Stop Being a Stumbling Block

"... make up your mind not to put any stumbling block
or obstacle in the way of a brother or sister"
(Romans 14:13, NIV).

In the early post-resurrection church, Christ-following Jews who were new and less mature in their faith were unaccepting of the freedom and grace introduced by Jesus in the New Covenant. They consequently became mired in non-essential traditions and legalistic practices of the Mosaic Law—such as what one could eat, drink, and wear—which caused discord and disunity among more mature Christians.

This precipitated the Apostle Paul's message to mature Christians in Romans 14:13 (above), in which he implored them to avoid practicing newfound freedoms under grace if they unwittingly caused new believers, who still practiced tenets of the law, to become conflicted and fall away from their faith. In other words, don't become a stumbling block or an obstacle to someone else.

The same advice aptly applies to how we should conduct ourselves in the presence of our loved ones. Permit me to describe a few stumbling blocks that Chris encountered, and one other experienced by a friend of mine.

****

One day when Chris was 18 and already in the grips of alcohol addiction, his mother discovered over 40 empty beer cans and liquor bottles hidden in his bedroom. As mortified as we were at this finding, it paled in comparison to us learning, many years later, that an adult relative had been supplying Chris and his friends with much of their alcohol—all in an attempt to "be their friend."

Unfortunately, we can't keep our loved ones in a protective bubble. Nonetheless, I think it's reasonable—indeed, sometimes necessary—to privately implore friends and family members to avoid partaking in any activity that might trigger our loved ones' addictive behavior.

But prepare yourself for pushback, especially among friends and family members who consume alcohol or drugs themselves. They may feel suspending their own substance use, even in the presence of your loved one, may be too big a sacrifice, and resent you for suggesting it.

****

When Chris was around nineteen, he got a part-time job with a telemarketing company while attending technical college. During the week of Christmas, the owners celebrated their successful sales season by leaving a bottle of liquor on each employee's desk for a job well done. You can imagine what happened next.

****

When Chris was in his mid-twenties, he'd been sober for about a month and I was just beginning to feel cautiously optimistic. Then one afternoon he called to tell me, in very slurred speech, that he had "messed up." Turned out some "friends" gave him a brownie laced with an unknown substance, which Chris claimed to have no foreknowledge of. Regardless of whether he did or didn't know, his friends, with full knowledge of Chris's addiction, willfully contributed to his relapse.

****

Finally, there was a man in his 50s who attended a recovery group I led at my church. After years of alcoholism, Carl (not his real name) became sober and had achieved two years of sobriety. But then his wife confided to him that she really missed the two of them being able to "kick back and share a drink together."

That was all the incentive he needed to abandon his sobriety and begin drinking a glass of wine each night to appease his wife. He insisted it was "all under control and he knew when to stop." While it may have been under control for the time being, I would place the odds of him being successful in controlling his addiction long-term to be somewhere between little to none, which is precisely what I told him.

****

So now comes the hard question: Are you or others in your loved one's life a stumbling block to their recovery? Be honest.

Perhaps the stumbling block you represent is different than the ones I've described. In fact, there are numerous ways you can unwittingly be contributing to your loved one's addiction. Let's discuss a couple.

Do you supply your loved one with money to purchase alcohol or drugs? It may ostensibly be for innocent purposes, like help with rent, food, cellphone bill, etc., but too often gets diverted into addictive substances. Stop being a stumbling block to their recovery! Next time you deem it appropriate to be generous (and be discerning whether it's appropriate to do so), make sure you're not unwittingly providing resources for drugs or alcohol.

Another way of being a stumbling block to your loved one is by projecting a negative and critical spirit toward them. Guard your tongue and avoid spewing things like: "Stop wasting your life!" "You're never going to get sober!" "When are you going to stop using?" "You're such a loser!"

Such venting only serves to heap shame on a loved one by lowering their self-esteem and raising their propensity for relapse—not to mention causing long-term damage to your relationship. These sentiments can also be communicated non-verbally through outward expressions of disgust and disappointment.

Remember, what you say or do in the presence of your loved one will either inspire and uplift, or discourage and condemn.

Choose wisely—and don't be a stumbling block!

TAKEAWAY:

Remove any potential stumbling blocks, such as access to alcohol or drugs you may possess, that could cause your loved one to relapse. Then encourage other family members and friends of your loved one to do the same.

GOD'S WORD:

"It is good not to eat meat or to drink wine, or to do anything by which your brother stumbles" (Romans 14:21, NIV).

PRAYER:

Lord, help us to avoid saying or doing things that would cause us to be stumbling blocks to our loved ones, and thus prolong their addiction.

Amen.

QUESTIONS:

1. Are you or others in your loved one's life a stumbling block to their recovery? If so, how?

2. How do you feel about talking to your loved one's friends and other family members about not being a stumbling block?

3. What specific behavior change can you make, if any, to avoid becoming a stumbling block to your loved one's recovery?

Day 11:

Stop Losing Your Balance

*"... Moses was settling disputes among the people, and he
was kept busy from morning till night. Then Jethro said, 'You
are not doing this right. You will wear yourself out and these
people as well. This is too much for you to do alone'"
(Exodus 18:13, 17-18, GNT).*

Jethro was a priest of Midian who also happened to be
Moses' father-in-law. When Jethro saw Moses becoming
burned out trying to do everything himself, he offered him
practical advice on how to work smarter—not harder—in order
to maintain balance in his life.

Similarly, allowing the wellbeing of our loved ones to
consume our thoughts can cause our lives to lose balance.
When their addiction becomes our obsession, we quickly lose
perspective on other things that are important to us: our
physical, mental, and spiritual health; our relationships with
other friends and family members; and even performing our
day-to-day responsibilities—like being a productive employee,
paying bills on time, performing household chores, and the like.

There's an expression often attributed to parents of addicts
that says: "I'm only as happy as my least happy child." For the
broader audience reading this book, a variation might be: "I'll
only be happy when my loved one is sober or drug free." While
this may sound poetic and noble, we must resist it from
becoming true of our own lives. Our inability to maintain a
healthy life balance while loving an addict can metastasize an

already difficult family situation into something far worse. It's also an unfair burden to place on your loved one.

In "Day 2: "Stop Enabling", I described how Chris would sometimes call me when living in Santa Monica or Chicago, and demand money for things he could or should have been able to pay for himself, such as food, rent, electricity, and transportation.

What I didn't describe is how upended I became after receiving those calls. When our conversation ended, I would frequently enact "Operation Rescue Chris." This meant that after work, I would stop at a nearby ATM to withdraw cash … rush to the airport … get a ticket on the next flight to whichever city Chris was in … take a hotel van that was in close proximity to his apartment … take him to dinner … give him the cash he requested (usually more than he requested) … give him a hug … tell him I loved him … hear him say he loved me, along with his promise, "This will never happen again, Dad"… take the hotel limo back to the airport … take the red-eye flight back home … and head straight to my office the next morning, hoping neither my boss nor coworkers would notice me wearing the same clothes as the day before. The entire episode left me exhausted.

(I should disclose that my wife was a flight attendant at the time, so I was able to fly for free using her travel benefits. Nonetheless, it still made for a harrowing 15-hour ordeal.)

I forget how many times I subjected myself to that bizarre ritual. Oh sure, I could have sent the money electronically. But whenever Chris was in trouble, I compulsively had to rescue him in person to make sure he was okay. It was the only way I could fool myself into thinking the problem had been solved (it wasn't) and things would get better (they didn't), not to mention making that knot in my stomach go away.

Needless to say, I had difficulty focusing on anything other than Chris's addiction. Meanwhile, other things, important things, weren't getting done—or at least not with any degree of excellence. That's what a life that's out of balance looks like. So let's explore some solutions.

Maintaining a Healthy Life Balance While Loving an Addict

Protect your physical, mental, and spiritual health:

- If you are physically able, carve out 15-30 minutes a day for exercise. You'll burn off a lot of stress, think with more clarity, and feel enormously better.

- Stay mentally engaged by pursuing a hobby, reading a book, seeing a movie, or volunteering for something you are passionate about.

- Attend church every Sunday, join a small group or consider forming your own "Loved Ones of Addicts" support group, read the Bible and a daily devotional (e.g., "Our Daily Bread"), meet with a Christian counselor.

Protect your relationships with other friends and family members:

- Be careful not to ignore relationships with other family members and friends. Be especially sensitive to giving small children the love and attention they need.

- Don't allow your loved one to become your sole topic of conversation with others. Remember, they have problems, too.

- Be considerate of well-meaning friends who have all the answers on what you should do about your loved one. Chances are, they've never walked in your shoes.

Perform your day-to-day responsibilities:

- Don't allow your loved one's addiction to become an excuse for not pulling your own weight at work or home. Resist succumbing to inertia. It will only make you feel worse.

- Strive for excellence in all that you do. Not only will it boost your self-esteem, but it will safeguard you from feeling sorry for yourself.

- If you find yourself becoming incapacitated in performing daily tasks due to anxiety over your loved one, you may be depressed. Seek professional help from a qualified Christian counselor.

It is not God's will that your life be out-of-balance due to your loved one's addiction. Neither is it His will that your happiness be solely contingent on your loved one's sobriety. You instead must limit and compartmentalize the extent to which your loved one's issues occupy your consciousness. Then devote your remaining attention to pursuing a balanced life—*an abundant life!*—that God has promised you. "I came that they may have life and have it abundantly" (John 10:10, ESV).

TAKEAWAY:

Don't allow your loved one's need for sobriety to become your all-consuming obsession. And don't deny yourself permission to be happy until they first achieve sobriety. Their need for sobriety is their responsibility—don't make it yours. Focus on things only you can control, like living a healthy, balanced life in the present.

GOD'S WORD:

"People ruin their lives by their own foolishness and then are angry at the Lord" (Proverbs 19:3, NLT).

PRAYER:

Heavenly Father, help us to maintain a healthy life balance between caring for our loved ones and protecting our own health and wellbeing.

Amen.

QUESTIONS:

1. Is your loved one's addiction causing you to feel your life is out of balance? If so, share some examples why.

2. Does this statement describe your life: "I'll only be happy when my loved one is sober or drug free." If so, how come?

3. From the suggestions provided in "Maintaining a Healthy Life Balance While Loving an Addict," what are some action steps you will take to restore more control and balance in your life?

Day 12:

Stop the Roller Coaster

"... without faith it is impossible to please God"
(Hebrews 11:6, NIV).

During the early years of Chris's addiction, whenever he spent time in an ER, jail, or courtroom, I remember feeling somewhat relieved, thinking, *Surely this time he's hit bottom and will turn his life around.* I assumed (prematurely) that Chris had seen the error of his ways, would get himself sober, and life could go back to normal.

Of course, Chris helped encourage this thinking by assuring us this was the case. As I shared in "Day 6: Stop Bailing," sometimes these incidents can be the impetus for an addict to embrace sobriety. But it usually doesn't happen that way. It didn't for Chris.

Riding the emotional roller coaster between euphoric hope (when you assume your loved one has hit bottom and will turn his life around) and crushing disappointment (when you realize it didn't happen) is all too common.

For Chris, it wasn't a single episode that turned him around. It was the cumulative effect of feeling "sick and tired of being sick and tired" (his words, not mine) after 18 years of hard drinking, coupled with mounting legal and financial consequences. He finally embraced the mindset, quite correctly, that there had to be a better way to live. If Chris ever did "hit bottom," I guess that was it. But instead of "bottoming out," it was more like an "epiphany."

So what do you do in the interim? Waiting for your loved one to become sober can seem like an eternity. You may even become cynical and defeatist in your attitude and outlook. Left unchecked, you may begin thinking God has forgotten you, and lose faith that your loved one will ever find sobriety.

This is when you need to step back, take a deep breath, and be reminded that this trial—like any other trial—will only be resolved by God, through God, and in God's perfect timing, not yours.

Once you've lost faith that your loved one will ever become sober, you've reached your own bottom. When that occurs, it becomes evident in your speech, your facial expressions, and your entire countenance. You can't hide it. And when your loved one senses that you and others have lost faith that they will ever get better, it only amplifies the guilt and shame they already feel, potentially driving them to consume even more substances to mask their hurt.

It's a vicious cycle.

Never lose faith that your loved one will one day become sober. To lose faith essentially means you've given up on God—which is never acceptable. Remember, " ... without faith it is impossible to please God ..." (Hebrews 11:6, NIV).

I found the following technique an effective way to stay focused on God's unconditional love and perfect timing during Chris's addiction.

Keeping a Godly Focus While Loving an Addict

1. **Live one day at a time**

   "Live one day at a time" isn't just a phrase used by addicts; it's for people like us, too. If your loved one is sober today, give God all the praise for His faithfulness without worrying about tomorrow. Remember Jesus' own words: "Therefore do not worry about tomorrow, for tomorrow will worry about itself. Each day has enough trouble of its own" (Matthew 6:34, NIV).

2. **Live from an eternal perspective**

   As Christ followers, we can take "Live one day at a time" a step further—by doing so from an *eternal perspective*. Remember the Apostle Paul's promise that "our light and momentary troubles are achieving for us an eternal glory that far outweighs them all" (2 Corinthians 4:17, NIV).

   By viewing today's problems from the perspective of a Christ-filled eternity we've all been promised, they somehow seem smaller, more manageable, and not quite so daunting. God will one day wipe away our tears—forever and ever more. Embrace that promise today! "He will wipe every tear from their eyes. There will be no more death or mourning or crying or pain, for the old order of things has passed away" (Revelation 21:4, NIV).

3. **Substitute worrisome thoughts with Godly thoughts**
   An important truth I came to realize far too late in life
   is this: 99% of the things we worry about—I mean
   really worry about—never come to pass.

   When worrisome thoughts enter your mind, discipline
   yourself to replace them with God's promise to "be
   close to the brokenhearted" and that He "saves those
   who are crushed in spirit" (Psalm 34:18, NIV).

Life has more than its share of *actual* problems without
adding *potential* problems to the mix. By not dwelling on
potential problems, you'll be more clear-headed to discern
God's will for effectively resolving (or coping with) the actual
problems when they arise.

> *If you look at the world, you'll be distressed.*
> *If you look within, you'll be depressed.*
> *If you look at God, you'll be at rest.*
> *- Corrie Ten Boom*

Step off the emotional roller coaster and stay focused on God!

TAKEAWAY:

Don't lose faith in your loved one finding sobriety. Once they sense that you've given up on them ever overcoming their addiction, it will only amplify the guilt and shame they already feel, potentially driving them to consume even more substances to mask their hurt. Focus instead on showing them unconditional love and support, while trusting in God's perfect timing.

GOD'S WORD:

" ... but those who hope in the Lord will renew their strength. They will soar on wings like eagles; they will run and not grow weary, they will walk and not be faint" (Isaiah 40:31, NIV).

PRAYER:

Heavenly Father, help us to avoid making premature assumptions that our loved ones will embrace sobriety. Let us focus instead on your sovereign control and perfect timing.

Amen.

QUESTIONS:

1. Have you ever been on the "emotional roller coaster" of first assuming your loved one had bottomed out and would embrace recovery, only to be disappointed a short time later? If so, describe the emotions you felt?

2. Do you encourage your loved one with the belief that they can become substance free? Or do you project pessimism, and the belief that it will never happen? Which of the two responses are more God-honoring?

3. Do you think the three steps suggested in "Keeping a Godly Focus While Loving an Addict" would help keep you off the emotional roller coaster? Why or why not?

Day 13:

Stop the Pity Party

"See to it ... that no bitter root grows up
to cause trouble and defile many"
(Hebrews 12:15, NIV).

L uke writes in his gospel of a bitter root that began festering in a woman named Martha soon after Jesus and His disciples arrived at her home for a visit. He begins describing the story in this familiar passage:

"As Jesus and his disciples were on their way, he came to a village where a woman named Martha opened her home to him. She had a sister called Mary, who sat at the Lord's feet listening to what he said. But Martha was distracted by all the preparations that had to be made" (Luke 10:38-40a, NIV).

Martha was annoyed with her sister, Mary, whom she thought was shirking her duties in helping prepare food for Jesus and His disciples. When Martha's resentment and bitterness finally boiled over, she pleaded to Jesus' sense of fairness:

"She [Martha] came to him and asked, 'Lord, don't you care that my sister has left me to do the work by myself? Tell her to help me'" (Luke 10:40b, NIV)!

Can you empathize with Martha's frustration when you feel exasperated by your loved one's addiction? Do you resent how it makes you feel? How the sacrifices you've made have not produced fruit? How you have been manipulated? Lied to?

Stolen from? If so, it's easy for a spirit of bitterness to take root in your language, attitude, and demeanor.

I remember having feelings of bitterness when talking to parents of "normal" adult children at work or social gatherings. When they inquired about my kids, I would quickly gloss over Chris's situation and instead ask about their children, which usually led to them sharing about their academic and professional pursuits—thus leaving me feel jealous, resentful ... and yes ... bitter.

There were also occasions during Chris's addiction when I had opportunities to advance in my career. But they invariably required longer hours and frequent overnight travel, so I elected not to pursue them, citing Chris's addiction as the reason why.

What if he gets a DUI or goes to the ER when I'm out of town? I wouldn't be there to help! What then?

My pity party had officially begun. Just like Martha complaining to Jesus about Mary, I wanted to shout: "Lord, why must *my* son be the one with an addiction? Why can't I just have a normal family without Chris's addiction consuming my time, attention, and resources?"

I soon learned that nothing sows the seeds of bitterness and self-pity more pervasively than comparing one's own life to the "perfect life" we perceive others lead. Such comparing doesn't change a thing—it just robs us of joy.

Jesus' response to Martha was—and still is—the perfect antidote to the comparison trap that fosters bitterness and self-pity:

"Martha, Martha," the Lord answered, "you are worried and upset about many things, but few things are needed—or indeed only one. Mary has chosen what is better, and it will not be taken away from her" (Luke 10:41-42, NIV).

Jesus reminds Martha (and us by extension) that He should be our primary focus. That our relationship with Him should be so "front and center" in our hearts and minds that we're not the least bit inclined to compare ourselves with others. Or, if we do, it's quickly squelched by the prompting of God's indwelling Spirit.

Martha was preoccupied with impressing Jesus and her other houseguests. If she wasn't the perfect host, she thought it might reflect poorly on her and her family. But her insatiable need for approval eclipsed her servant's heart. Which is why Jesus commended Mary for choosing the "one thing necessary," the "good portion," instead of assisting Martha with the meal. Mary was more interested in the spiritual food Jesus was sharing, which was eternal, rather than the physical food that Martha was fretting over, which was temporal.

Whereas Martha's bitterness toward Mary emanated from having to prepare dinner by herself, my bitterness toward Chris emanated from the intrusion his addiction had become on my life. At the core of our mutual bitterness was a fear of being embarrassed that others (from more "perfect" families) might think less of us.

But a verse in Galatians served as the perfect wakeup call to my twisted thinking. The Apostle Paul wrote: "Am I now trying to win the approval of human beings, or of God? Or am I trying to please people? If I were still trying to please people, I would not be a servant of Christ" (Galatians 1:10, NIV).

Once I recovered from my "comparison-itis" and refocused myself on the Lord, I adopted an entirely different approach to talking with others about Chris. No longer would I gloss over his addiction and change the subject. Instead, I'd say, "My son, Chris, is currently struggling with an alcohol addiction, but we love him dearly and we're trusting God to help guide him to a life of sobriety."

I was amazed how often my candor about Chris's addiction prompted others to share about someone in their lives experiencing a similar struggle. Mutual prayer for our loved ones would often ensue.

Has your loved one's addiction caused you to compare yourself with others who seemingly don't have such life issues? Have you become bitter as a result? If so, Jesus gave us the perfect remedy for ending our pity party: Look upward! Focus instead on God's amazing love, grace, forgiveness, and sovereignty. Take time to be still in the Lord's presence and nourished by His Word. "Therefore, holy brothers and sisters, partners in the heavenly calling, fix your thoughts on Jesus, whom we acknowledge as our apostle and high priest" (Hebrews 3:1, NIV).

TAKEAWAY:

Don't become bitter and resentful at how your loved one's addiction has affected your life. Neither should you compare yourself to "more perfect" families who don't have an addict, or worry what they may think about you and your family. The favor you seek is from the Lord, not others.

GOD'S WORD:

"Finally, brothers and sisters, whatever is true, whatever is noble, whatever is right, whatever is pure, whatever is lovely, whatever is admirable—if anything is excellent or praiseworthy—think about such things" (Philippians 4:8, NIV).

PRAYER:

Holy Spirit, speak to our hearts if we feel a "root of bitterness" forming against our loved ones. Help us not to compare ourselves with others who blessedly don't have a loved one who struggles with addiction.

Amen.

QUESTIONS:

1. Do you ever compare yourself to other families where no addiction exists, and experience feelings of jealousy and resentment? If so, does it lead you to feeling bitter toward your loved one?

2. As a Christ follower, how does Galatians 1:10 help re-center your thinking about comparing yourself to other "more perfect" people and families? "Am I now trying

to win the approval of human beings, or of God? Or am I trying to please people? If I were still trying to please people, I would not be a servant of Christ" (Galatians 1:10, NIV).

3. Going forward, how will you describe your loved one to others when asked?

Day 14:

Stop Going It Alone

"A man who isolates himself seeks his own desire;
He rages against all wise judgment"
(Proverbs 18:1, NKJV).

The emotional response we have to our loved one's addiction can encompass many feelings: guilt, shame, anxiety, despair, and anger. Which is why the love and support of your family, pastor, and friends can be extremely beneficial—especially if any of them have experienced a similar struggle with one of their loved ones.

Like any other crisis, it's never wise to go it alone. To that end, listed below are some support resources I would recommend for loved ones of addicts:

Christian Therapist

I've alluded several times to seeing a Christian therapist for help with my codependency issues. That relationship began at the insistence of my wife, Nancie (Chris's stepmother), who observed that my obsessing and enabling over Chris was spiraling out of control. She thought that a Christian therapist could help me see how my behavior was actually hurting, not helping, Chris—and by extension, herself, my daughter, and stepdaughter.

Just before my first session ended, the therapist said something that changed my life: "Jon, in a non-literal sense, you are as much of an addict as your son is. (Boy, did that get my attention!) Just as your son uses alcohol to make his pain and anxiety go away, you use money, as your 'drug of choice,' to solve his problems—albeit temporarily—and to make your pain and anxiety go away. You do it to untie that knot you feel in your stomach every time your son gets into trouble. And you do it to make your own self feel better. Your enabling is exacerbating your son's addiction by allowing him to avoid consequences. You need to get out of the way of God performing His redemptive work in your son."

I was guilty as charged, of course, and remained in weekly therapy for about a year, learning all about codependency, boundaries, and the need for consequences in Chris's life.

My most difficult awakening came when my therapist told me, in as gentle a way as he knew how, that if he had a hundred patients like Chris, he would expect only a few to survive. I initially thought it was horrifically cruel of him to say such a thing. But he was wisely preparing me (to the extent anyone could ever prepare me) for the possible, even probable, loss of my son to alcoholism.

By helping me process my worst-case scenario mentally, emotionally, and spiritually—in advance of it ever occurring—I learned to fully trust and rest in God's sovereignty more deeply than ever before.

Without a doubt, had I not sought the counsel of a Christian therapist, I don't know if Nancie and I would still be married, or whether Chris would yet be sober.

If you feel your life is spiraling out of control due to your loved one's addiction, don't hesitate to seek the counsel of a licensed Christian therapist, ideally one who also has LADC (licensed alcohol drug abuse counselor) credentials.

Al-Anon (www.al-anon.org)

When I began Christian therapy for codependency, my therapist strongly urged me to attend an Al-Anon support group. I'm glad he did.

Al-Anon is a "mutual support group of peers who share their experience in applying the Al-Anon principles to problems related to the effects of a problem drinker in their lives." (Al-Anon Meetings, n.d.) They follow their own version of the 12 Steps (similar to Alcoholics Anonymous), and their meetings are led by a facilitator who leads the group in readings and a time of sharing.

Like Alcoholics Anonymous, Al-Anon is a spiritual fellowship, not a religious one. They readily welcome members of all faiths (or none), but refrain from discussing specific religious doctrines, including Christianity.

The entirety of the Al-Anon 12 Steps makes seven references to God without identifying any particular one. If you are able to mentally transpose those seven references to God as being Jesus Christ whenever you read or hear them, you can derive much value from an Al-Anon Family Group. They do an exemplary job of educating attendees about codependency, specifically as it relates to loved ones of alcoholics.

With more than 24,000 Al-Anon groups nationally, there are undoubtedly one or more groups in proximity to you. In fact, if you are experiencing extreme anguish due to your loved one's alcoholism, you could potentially attend multiple Al-Anon meetings each week in most large cities.

Al-Anon also provides Alateen meetings, which are "peer support groups for teens who are struggling with the effects of someone else's problem drinking." (Resources for Professionals, n.d.)

Both Al-Anon and Alateen meeting locations can be found at www.al-anon.org/al-anon-meetings.

Nar-Anon (www.nar-anon.org)

Nar-Anon is similar to Al-Anon in that they are 12-Step oriented and spiritually based (i.e. they discuss God generically as a Higher Power without mention of specific religious doctrines), but are primarily—though not exclusively—focused on families and friends of drug addicts as opposed to alcoholics. You can find a meeting nearest you by going to www.nar-anon.org/find-a-meeting. They also have meetings for teens in their Narateen program (information at www.nar-anon.org).

Celebrate Recovery (www.celebraterecovery.com)

Celebrate Recovery (CR) is a Christ-centered, 12-Step program of Pastor Rick Warren's Saddleback Church in Lake Forest, California. Founded by John Baker, CR holds weekly meetings in more than 35,000 churches throughout the U.S., and even more internationally. CR targets anyone struggling with addiction, codependency, or any other "hurt, habit, or hang-up."

The format of most CR meetings includes a large group meeting where attendees gather together for music, a reading of the CR 12 Steps and 8 Principles, followed by open share groups and step groups. Many meetings provide a meal beforehand.

Be aware that the CR small group you attend might include people with a variety of issues different than your own. The location of the CR meeting nearest to you can be found at: www.celebraterecovery.com/crgroups.

Codependents Anonymous (www.coda.org)

Codependents Anonymous (CoDa) is a 12-step recovery program designed to help people develop functional, healthy relationships. The only membership requirement is to want loving relationships and to move beyond personal histories. Members are encouraged to build a relationship with a higher power. They offer four types of meetings: speaker meetings, open share meetings, topic share meetings, and tradition study meetings.

****

Every support group has its own distinct style and personality. If you have a disappointing experience with one, try another. Keep attending different groups until you find one you feel comfortable with. Once you do, you'll agree it's well worth it.

Finally, be sure to read the chapter "Starting a 'Loved Ones of Addicts' Support Group"!

TAKEAWAY:

Don't struggle alone with the hurt and pain of your loved one's addiction. Seek out a support group and/or qualified professional to help sustain you through their addiction journey. Draw close to the Lord through daily prayer and a quiet time of Bible study and devotion.

GOD'S WORD:

"Do not forsake wisdom, and she will protect you; love her, and she will watch over you" (Proverbs 4:6, NIV).

PRAYER:

Lord, guide us in finding supportive resources that will help us to cope with our loved ones' addiction.

Amen.

QUESTIONS:

1. Have you been "going it alone" in coping with your loved one's addiction? If yes, how's that been working for you? If no, what other resources have you utilized?

2. After reading this chapter, what other resources might you explore to find additional support?

3. Are you reluctant to attend a CR, Al-Anon, Nar-Anon, or CODA group? If so, what is your biggest reason?

Day 15:

Stop Being Unforgiving

"Jesus said, 'Father, forgive them, for they
do not know what they are doing'"
(Luke 23:34, NIV).

There Jesus hung … nailed to a cross, gasping for breath—bleeding, beaten, flogged, thirsty, and naked— watching His captors divide up his torn garments by casting lots, the modern day equivalent of flipping a coin or shaking dice.

Yet despite His agony and humiliation, Jesus pleaded with His Father to forgive them, for they knew not what they were doing. What an amazing demonstration of God's love, grace, and compassion!

Are we as quick to extend Christ-like forgiveness to our loved ones when their poor choices cause us hurt or harm? Even when they do so repeatedly? Perhaps you've been lied to. Stolen from. Or traumatized by your loved one's hospitalizations and incarcerations … to name a few. And you ask, "God wants me to forgive all that?"

Yep, He does. And forgive we must. Why? Because God commands it: "Forgive as the Lord forgave you" (Colossians 3:13, NIV). It means surrendering your claim to resentment and letting go of the anger.

There's a popular expression that says: "Refusing to forgive is like trying to hurt someone by drinking poison" (original author unknown). Mark Twain wrote, "Anger is an acid that can do more harm to the vessel in which it is stored than to anything on which it is poured." The message is clear: We only hurt ourselves—not our loved ones—by refusing to extend them forgiveness, and harboring anger instead.

Forgiveness is unilaterally letting go of a past offense that someone committed against you, regardless of whether that person has apologized and requested forgiveness.

Some of us have been hurt so deeply by our loved ones that the thought of forgiving them—especially without first receiving their apology—seems untenable. But consider this: Did the men who crucified Jesus extend Him any apologies before He asked His Father to forgive them? No. In fact, they were still in the act of crucifying Him on the cross when He did.

I was profoundly hurt and angered for many years by Chris's alcohol-related behavior. Over time, my anger became almost debilitating. And I knew, as a Christ follower, that I was out-of-step in my walk with the Lord. God seemed distant and detached from me. Truth be told, I was mad at Him, too. I often thought, *Why did You allow my son to be an alcoholic in the first place? Don't you realize how anguishing this is to me?*

It had been a long time since I felt "the peace of God, which transcends all understanding, will guard your hearts and your minds in Christ Jesus" (Philippians 4:7, NIV). Deep down, I knew the only cure for my anger was to extend Chris my unconditional forgiveness.

But simply resolving to forgive Chris left me feeling inadequate, like I was only reciting words and going through the motions. I prayed repeatedly for God to give me the desire and will to truly forgive—but even those prayers fell short.

My breakthrough finally came when I adopted a four-step exercise to prepare my mind and spirit *before* praying to forgive Chris. It proved effective for me, and I hope it will for you as well.

Preparing to Pray the Prayer of Forgiveness

1. Reflect how God the Father, the eternal Creator of the universe, first forgave you. More specifically, how He loved you so much that He sacrificed His only Son, Jesus, so that your sins (and mine)—past, present, and future—could be forgiven; thus ascribing to you, a believer in Christ, the assurance of knowing when this life is over, you will immediately enter into His presence, and thereafter spend a joyous and pain-free eternity with Him in heaven. "For God so loved the world that he gave his one and only Son, that whoever believes in him shall not perish but have eternal life" (John 3:16, NIV).

2. Meditate intentionally on the torturous suffering Jesus endured so that you could be forgiven. Picture the Roman soldiers mocking Him, beating Him, spitting on Him, pulling out His beard, flogging Him, placing a crown of thorns on His head, and nailing His hands and feet to a cross. If Jesus is able to love and forgive those who did all that, how can we, in obedience to Him, not forgive our loved ones? "But God demonstrates his own love for us in this: While we were still sinners, Christ died for us" (Romans 5:8, NIV).

3. Place all the hurt your loved one has inflicted upon you alongside the suffering Jesus endured to forgive you of your sins. Regardless of your situation, your hurt pales in comparison. "But he was wounded for our

transgressions; he was crushed for our iniquities; upon him was the chastisement that brought us peace, and with his stripes we are healed" (Isaiah 53:5, ESV).

4. You now have the perspective to humbly and reverently approach the throne of God in a spirit of prayer, asking Him for the power to release any anger and resentment you may still harbor toward your loved one, and to fully and unconditionally, without reservation, extend your forgiveness. "Let my prayer be counted as incense before you, and the lifting up of my hands as the evening sacrifice" (Psalm 141:2, ESV)!

This exercise enabled me to step outside of my own self, reconnect with the Holy Spirit's indwelling presence, and view Chris's offenses through a spiritual lens that shifted my focus away from my own hurt to Christ's unfathomable sacrifice for my sins—a sacrifice for which God granted me (and you) forgiveness. This allowed me, for the first time, to extend Chris my heartfelt forgiveness for all the pain that I endured from his addiction.

It's my prayer that it will do the same for you.

TAKEAWAY:

Forgive your loved one of any hurt their addiction has caused you. Do not make your forgiveness contingent on them first apologizing to you. Make it a unilateral, Christ-like act of forgiveness that releases them from harboring any guilt or shame. Focus instead on the amazing sacrifice Christ made on the cross to make it possible for God to forgive you.

GOD'S WORD:

"For if you forgive other people when they sin against you, your heavenly Father will also forgive you. But if you do not forgive others their sins, your Father will not forgive your sins" (Matthew 6:14-15, NIV).

PRAYER:

Lord, release us of all anger and resentment toward our loved ones so that we can extend them our full and unconditional forgiveness—just as You forgave us.

Amen.

QUESTIONS:

1. Do you replay in your mind specific instances when your loved one hurt you? Does doing so make you feel better or worse?

2. Have you been unsuccessful in your attempts to forgive your loved one? If yes, how has that affected your mutual relationship? Your relationship with Christ?

3. Do you think the 4-Step exercise, "Preparing to Pray the Prayer of Forgiveness," could help you to fully and

unconditionally forgive your loved one? Why or why not?

Day 16:

Stop Thwarting a Reconciliation

*"If it is possible, as far as it depends on you,
live at peace with everyone"
(Romans 12:18, NIV).*

It's tempting to stay perpetually angry at an addicted loved one. We naively believe that the more shame, blame, and disappointment we project on them, the sooner they will come to their senses and get serious about sobriety.

But this behavior is counterproductive, and certainly inconsistent with Paul's teaching in Romans 12:18 (above).

I was angry during much of Chris's addiction journey, especially during trips to ERs when his blood alcohol content frequently exceeded .40. I mustered up the angriest demeanor I could to let him know, without words, just how incensed I was—not only with him, but other family members who exhibited a more consoling bedside manner. I preferred making him feel scorned and punished—not like things were "business as usual."

I later came to realize that addicts heap enough shame on themselves without others adding to it. And when they mess up, like going to the ER as a result of an overdose or binge drinking, we should project nothing less than a Christ-like countenance of love, care, compassion, and yes, forgiveness.

As we learned in the previous chapter, we must forgive our loved ones for the poor choices they've made, regardless of whether they've asked for it—not for their peace of mind, but our own. Once they formally apologize for their offenses and seek our forgiveness (which hopefully we've already extended to them), our relationship can progress to reconciliation.

Reconciliation often doesn't occur until a loved one is in a recovery program and has experienced a season of sobriety. In the 12 Steps of Alcoholics Anonymous, this happens in Step 8: "Made a list of all persons we had harmed, and became willing to make amends to them all." (Alcoholics Anonymous, 1939, 1955, 1976, 2001)

This is a vitally important milestone for you and your loved one. It's a sign that your relationship has progressed to a higher level of honesty and normalcy. It means the proverbial elephant in the room—i.e., those addiction-related incidents that caused so much division, hurt, pain, and anger—have finally been acknowledged, apologized for, forgiven, and turned over to God.

No, it's not a guarantee of smooth sailing in the future. There may be lapses, relapses, and missteps along the way. But hopefully it signals a stronger and more fortified relationship between the two of you—one that can endure the hurt and disappointment that addicts are prone to cause, which can lead to relational paralysis.

Chris arrived at this stage somewhere around 90 days of sobriety following his fourth rehab. He was in a high-accountability program offered by the county called DWI Court. Among other things, DWI Court subjected Chris to four-to-six random urine analysis checks per week (often in the middle of the night), documented attendance at four or more recovery meetings per week, a weekly meeting with his parole officer, a bi-weekly meeting with the DWI Court Judge, and an ignition interlock device installed on his vehicle once his driver's license was reinstated.

Most of those requirements gradually tapered off over a two-year period. But there was no gaming the system. A single infraction would land Chris in jail for months.

After 90 days in the DWI Court program, Chris actually started believing he could achieve sobriety. His newfound optimism became contagious, and soon extended to me and other family members. For the first time ever, Chris began keeping count of his own sober days—something he'd never done before, because doing so placed too much pressure on him not to disappoint us.

But it wasn't until shortly after Chris's two-year sober anniversary that I began to feel—for the first time in 18 years— real trust in our relationship.

Trust that I could answer his phone calls without hearing an intoxicated voice on the other end. Trust that I could meet him for coffee, dinner, or a baseball game without smelling alcohol on his breath. Trust that he wasn't going to drive while intoxicated and place his own life and others' lives in harm's way.

Indeed, Chris had worked hard to regain my trust. What a joy it was—*and still is*—to consider him trustworthy!

In retrospect, my newfound trust in Chris was merely an extension of the trust I placed in God for his sobriety: "Commit your way to the Lord; trust in him, and he will act" (Psalm 37:5, ESV).

Does trusting Chris mean that I no longer worry about him relapsing? Not exactly. It's just not something I dwell on anymore. But I'm realistic enough to know, on any given day, the risk of Chris relapsing is still present, no matter how infinitesimal the possibility may seem. Which is why, on most days, I still take a moment to briefly consider the possibility.

Doing so gives me a healthy sense of preparedness as I reflect on God's faithfulness during Chris's 18-year addiction. And because of God's past faithfulness, I can trust His future faithfulness should I ever revisit that dark valley again.

"And we know that in all things God works for the good of those who love him, who have been called according to his purpose" (Romans 8:28, NIV).

TAKEAWAY:

Make every effort to reconcile with your loved one once they apologize for their addiction-related choices and behavior. By continuing to project culpability onto them for past offenses, your relationship will never be fully reconciled, and mutual trust never achieved.

GOD'S WORD:

"Truly my soul finds rest in God;
my salvation comes from him.
Truly he is my rock and my salvation;
he is my fortress, I will never be shaken"
(Psalm 62:1-2, NIV).

PRAYER:

Lord, help us to reconcile with our loved ones once they apologize for their actions and seek our forgiveness—even if we've already extended it to them. Then guide us to correctly discern, by their demonstrated actions, when we can risk trusting them again.

Amen.

QUESTIONS:

1. Which stage are you in with your loved one? Forgiveness? Reconciliation? Trust? Or none of the above? If you're in the forgiveness or reconciliation stages, what needs to happen before you can advance to the next stage?

2. Have you ever tried "motivating" your loved one to become sober by projecting anger, guilt, disappointment, or shame? How did that work out?

3. Have you lost hope of ever regaining trust with your loved one? If so, what does that say about your trust in God?

Day 17:

Stop Fearing an Intervention

"If your brother or sister sins, go and point out their fault, just between the two of you. If they listen to you, you have won them over. But if they will not listen, take one or two others along, so that 'every matter may be established by the testimony of two or three witnesses"
(Matthew 18:15-16, NIV).

E ven though the above verse is directed at Christians who have been hurt or harmed by another Christian brother or sister, the remedy, nonetheless, is appropriate for everyone, regardless of whether their loved one is a Christ follower.

Chances are, you've already confronted your loved one (hopefully in a spirit of Christ-like love and humility) about their addiction and need for rehab. If they chose to disregard your concerns, the next step is to repeat the encounter with more people who share your concerns, and do so in a formal and structured encounter called an *intervention*.

Ironically, our family never conducted an intervention with Chris. There's really no particular reason why, other than his addiction was already the focus of most every discussion we had with him (inappropriately), so the prospect of an intervention may have seemed redundant.

The closest we ever came to an actual intervention occurred when Chris was in his early twenties. It quickly degenerated into a checklist of what not to do. His mother and I naively thought Chris would be less inclined to overreact or become angry if we confronted him in a public place, like a restaurant (Mistake #1). We strategically sat him on the window side of the booth, with his mother sitting next to him and me sitting across the table, thus cutting off his escape route and making ourselves his captive audience (Mistake #2). When we sternly began dictating the terms of him returning to treatment as a consequence for damaging his mother's car (Mistake #3), he lost it. He climbed up on the booth backrest, crawled behind his mother, and jumped onto the floor—creating quite the spectacle in the process. Within seconds he was out the door. There we sat, stunned and humiliated, while other customers pretended not to notice what had just transpired.

When done correctly, however, interventions can be effective in helping addicts to step out of their denial and understand the seriousness of their condition. By doing so, they come to realize how their self-destructive behavior is negatively affecting their loved ones, which hopefully persuades them to seek treatment by entering rehab.

Specifically, an intervention is a meeting that's been carefully planned by the addict's loved ones, ideally in consultation with a suitable health professional such as a doctor, licensed alcohol and drug counselor, professional interventionist, or a pastor with whom the addict knows and respects.

How an Intervention Works

Most interventions generally follow the process below:

Step 1:

- Identify a health professional to consult with and/or act as an interventionist at the intervention.

Step 2:

- Make a list of those closest to your loved one whose lives have been adversely affected by the addict's choices and behavior.

Step 3:

- From the list you've compiled, assemble an intervention team who will attend the intervention. The total number of participants should be kept relatively small— anywhere from four to six, not including the health professional. The danger in having more is that your loved one might feel outnumbered and ganged up on, causing less-than-truthful responses or a complete shutdown.

Step 4:

- With the help of your health professional, research local treatment or rehab programs and decide which one is most suitable for your loved one. Most inpatient rehabs will agree to make contingent arrangements for intaking a loved one immediately following a successful intervention.

Step 5:

- Decide who among those attending will speak at the intervention.

- Those speaking should write an intervention letter that they will read during the intervention. With humility and love, they should describe factual incidents where the loved one's choices and behavior created problems, without projecting shame or condemnation.

- Each letter should end with a heartfelt plea for the loved one to immediately enter treatment, along with specific actions (i.e. consequences) that will result for refusing to go.

Step 6:

- When ready for the intervention, the loved one should be invited to the intervention site without prior knowledge of what will occur. In the event the loved one responds with defiance and anger upon realizing the nature of the meeting, decide in advance who would be most capable of restoring calm and composure. Often this is the health professional along with a member of the intervention team with whom the loved one is particularly close to and respects.

- After warmly welcoming the loved one upon arriving at the intervention site, members of the intervention team take turns reading their letters, and expressing their concerns and feelings to the loved one.

- After all letters have been read, the loved one is extended the opportunity to be immediately transported to the treatment center to begin rehab.

In the event your loved one refuses treatment following an intervention, it's of utmost importance that you follow through on the consequences that were read in the letters. Allowing your loved one to think you were just "crying wolf" will only damage your own credibility, and diminish any future attempt to encourage treatment.

Finally, all members of an intervention team should accept their role very seriously. Humbly embrace Matthew 5:9 as your own: "Blessed are the peacemakers, for they will be called children of God" (NIV). God has a plan for this dear soul who has gone astray. And there is no doubt that He is calling you to help restore His child to sobriety and good health.

Be obedient to your calling.

TAKEAWAY:

Organize a well-planned intervention by forming an intervention team comprised of the loved one's friends and family members. If possible, include a health professional to help facilitate. Then, in a spirit of Christ-like love and humility, the team should confront the loved one about their need for immediate rehab, and the resulting consequences for not following-through.

GOD'S WORD:

"Let us therefore make every effort to do what leads to peace and to mutual edification" (Romans 14:19, NIV).

PRAYER:

Lord Jesus, we ask you to guide us in planning and executing our loved one's intervention so that it leads them to enter treatment and achieve lasting sobriety.

Amen.

QUESTIONS:

1. Have you ever attempted to hold an intervention for your loved one? If yes, how did it go? If no, are you more inclined to try after reading this chapter?

2. How do you think your loved one would react to a well-planned intervention? Who would you consider being on the intervention team? Would you include a health professional?

3. As a member of the intervention team, what consequences would you institute if your loved one refused to enter treatment following an intervention?

Day 18:

Stop Thinking All Rehabs Work

"He is not afraid of bad news; his heart is firm, trusting in the LORD"
(Psalm 112:7, ESV).

When our loved ones enter into a season of sobriety (or being substance free), it's natural for our hearts to swell with renewed hope and optimism. We can't help but wonder: *Is this it? Is our long nightmare over? Will life finally return to normal? How can we know for sure?*

We're probably never more optimistic than when our loved ones complete a rehab or treatment program. The longer the rehab, the higher our optimism. So we fervently pray that our loved ones have "bottomed out and turned the corner." And why wouldn't we? It's only reasonable.

In the midst of our excitement, however, we must never forget that lapses and relapses are often part of the recovery process, and not something to be overly shocked by if they occur. In fact, not to diminish their seriousness, but 40 to 60 percent of individuals in recovery experience a relapse. (Comparison of Relapse Rates Between Substance Use Disorders and Other Chronic Illnesses, 2000)

So let's define the difference between lapse and relapse. A lapse represents a temporary slip or return to a previous behavior that one is trying to control or quit (usually a onetime occurrence), whereas a relapse represents a full-blown return to

127

a pattern of behavior that one has been trying to moderate or quit altogether. (Marlatt, G. A. and Donovan, D. M., 2005)

As mentioned previously, Chris completed four rehabs during his 18-year addiction. His fourth rehab was immediately followed by an extended DWI Court program, which led to his current season of long-term sobriety (six years as of this writing – PRAISE GOD!).

My reaction to the relapses following Chris's first two rehabs was a crushing mixture of disappointment, anger, worry, and despair. But my reaction to the relapses following his third and fourth rehabs was primarily disappointment. The other emotions—anger, worry, and despair—were largely absent.

The reason? Through counseling and self-study, I had become better educated about codependency, and was better able to detach myself from taking responsibility for Chris's self-destructive decision-making.

It also helped that I had learned how to recognize when an impending relapse was about to occur, which made me infinitely more prepared when they happened. Let's explore those next.

Warning Signs of an Impending Relapse

Recognizing the warning signs of relapse in your loved one can help guard you emotionally when a relapse is imminent:

- Romanticizing previous alcohol or drug abuse

- Thinking one slip will be OK

- Lying and being dishonest

- Isolating from others

- Skipping therapy or support group meetings

- Interacting with friends or other people who drink or use drugs

(Elkins, Relapse & Slips: Warning Signs, Triggers & Prevention Plan, n.d.)

If you share open and healthy communication with your loved one about their addiction (as described in "Day 7: Stop Provoking"), you may consider sharing your observations. But only do so in a spirit of Christ-like love. Pray that they will "listen to advice and accept instruction, that [they] may gain wisdom in the future" (Proverbs 19:20, ESV).

The warning sign that Chris most often exhibited was "Interacting with friends or other people who drink or use drugs." It's always difficult for addicts to separate themselves from long-established, yet unsafe friendships and relationships. Which is why creating a new social network of safe and sober-minded people is integral to them achieving long-term recovery.

The Three Stages of Relapse

Addiction professionals generally concur that relapse is more a process than a singular decision to resume using. It manifests itself in three consecutive stages:

1. Emotional Relapse:
   - Begins to consider using again

   - Experiences negative feelings, such as anger, moodiness and anxiousness

   - May display inconsistent eating and sleeping habits

- Not using addiction support systems (i.e. meetings, sponsor, safe friends, etc.)

2. Mental Relapse:
- Experiences strong internal struggle between desire to maintain long-term sobriety and to resume using again

- Eventually begins seriously thinking about using again—sometimes obsessively

3. Physical Relapse:
- The addict actually consumes the substance and breaks their sobriety

(Melemis, Sept 1988)

When a loved one relapses, it often triggers intense cravings to continue using again, thus risking a return to consistent substance abuse. Which is why it's crucially important for loved ones to immediately return to rehab following a relapse. But they often resist doing so, choosing instead (to the dismay of family and friends) to embark on another season of addiction.

HALT

Halt is an easy-to-remember acronym commonly used in recovery circles. It stands for Hungry, Angry, Lonely, and Tired. If an addict is experiencing one or more of these feelings, they can become susceptible to self-destructive behavior, including relapse. If you observe them in your loved one, heed them as an early warning signal. Share what you're seeing and ask what you can do to help.

Relapse Prevention Plan

Once your loved one enters into a season of sobriety, it would be wise to provide them a relapse prevention plan (normally part of any credible drug or alcohol rehab), which should always be accessible and contain the following information:

- Someone to call

- A safe place to go

- A list of personal reasons for staying sober

- Examples of stress relief strategies

- A schedule of local support group meetings

- Hotline numbers or crisis lines

- Locations of emergency services

(Elkins, Relapse & Slips: Warning Signs, Triggers & Prevention Plan, n.d.)

If a Relapse Occurs

It bears repeating: lapses and relapses are often part of the recovery process. But the way in which you act toward your loved one in the event of a relapse is of paramount importance. Remember, addicts heap enough shame on themselves without you or others piling on to make them feel even more hopeless. "Therefore, there is now no condemnation for those who are in Christ Jesus" (Romans 8:1, NIV).

If your loved one relapses, respond in a manner that only exemplifies unconditional, Christ-like love and compassion. Remind them frequently that they're not a failure, and that the progress they've made thus far is both credible and real. Then encourage them to immediately return to rehab and get back on track, and that you'll be waiting for them on the other side— with open arms.

TAKEAWAY:

Don't assume that your loved one's completion of rehab is a guarantee of long-term sobriety. Lapses and relapses may occur, so manage your expectations accordingly. Prepare yourself by knowing the warning signs of an impending relapse. If a relapse happens, affirm your loved one's prior progress and encourage an immediate return to rehab.

GOD'S WORD:

"God is our refuge and strength, an ever-present help in trouble. Therefore, we will not fear..." (Psalm 46:1-2, NIV).

PRAYER:

Lord Jesus, guard our emotions and words should our loved ones ever relapse after completing rehab. Help us to encourage and persuade them to return to rehab and resume a life of sobriety.

Amen.

QUESTIONS:

If your loved one is in a season of sobriety...

1. Are you observing any of the warning signs of a pending relapse?

2. Would your loved one be receptive to you sharing about the warning signs you are observing?

3. Where is your loved one in "The Three Stages of Relapse"?

4. Do you feel better equipped now to handle the emotional pain of your loved one relapsing than when you started reading this book? Why?

Day 19:

Stop Selecting the Wrong Rehab Part 1

"The way of a fool is right in his own eyes,
but the wise listen to others"
(Proverbs 12:15, NLT).

Since Jesus' death almost two-thousand years ago, people have largely ignored the Scriptural warnings of His Second Coming, which will lead to judgment for the ungodly. Matthew's Gospel likens those in denial of the Second Coming to those who scoffed at Noah for building the ark: "...they did not understand until the flood came and took them all away; so will the coming of the Son of Man be" (Matthew 24:39, NASB).

Similarly, when an addict's heart is hardened to the reality of their present condition, they are, like those who deny Christ's imminent return, steeped in denial, and foolishly allowing pride to direct their path and determine their destiny. They are out of sync with God's plan for their life.

Which is why, before most addicts become sober, they must step out of their denial and seek counsel from those who are qualified to help them. This normally requires completion of a rehab (or treatment) program, which is integral to them becoming sober. Rehab equips them with the knowledge and coping skills necessary to overcome their addiction.

At some point, you may become involved in selecting or recommending a rehab program for your loved one. This can be a sensitive subject, which many of the addict's friends and family members have strong opinions about. So my non-expert opinions are just that—my own opinions, based solely on my personal experience with Chris and from working with other addicts.

To me, the biggest determining factor of whether an addict will succeed in rehab is how they view their present condition. Specifically, does your loved one (1) acknowledge the existence of their addiction (no doubt the result of experiencing hard consequences), and (2) admit being powerless to overcome it in their own strength? If not, I submit the likelihood of a successful rehab, especially the first time, to be somewhat minimal, and you should manage your expectations accordingly.

Does this mean that an addict who's in denial should not go to rehab? Absolutely not. It merely suggests the addict is going for an alternative reason. Perhaps an intervention by family and friends created a guilty conscience but not an acknowledgement of their addiction. Or there's a court order to enter rehab as consequence for a DUI or probation violation.

Regardless, an addict entering rehab for the wrong reason is less likely to achieve sobriety. There's nothing wrong with being hopeful, but just remain guarded about their prospects for long-term success—at least for the time being.

Chris's mother and I forced him into his first rehab while he was still a minor, knowing he would resist going once he became an adult. When he walked out of rehab 30 days later, we had high hopes his addiction was defeated. But four months later, we were crushed when he suffered a relapse.

It's important not to view unsuccessful rehabs as a waste of time and money. I believe that each of Chris's four rehabs, in different ways, helped prepare him for his eventual sobriety.

Next, let's review some other considerations in selecting the best rehab for an addict. The first thing to understand is not all rehabs are alike, which is why this chapter and the next will overview some key considerations when making this decision.

Faith-based or Not

Many Christians passionately argue that the best hope any addict has for sobriety is by entering a Christ-centered treatment program, where hopefully they will receive Christ as their Savior and become substance free. Since this is a Christ-centered book written largely for a Christian audience, many will undoubtedly assume that I agree.

But I concur only if the addict already professes to be a Christ follower, or is at least receptive to undergoing treatment in a faith-based program. Addicts who are openly resistant or hostile to the Gospel message would, in my opinion, be better served in a secular program.

Within the context of God's sovereignty, every addict who achieves sobriety only does so by the grace of God, whether they realize it or not. That being said, I've witnessed numerous addicts find full and lasting sobriety in both Christian and non-Christian rehabs.

If your loved one is highly resistant to the Gospel, don't outright reject directing them to a secular treatment program. They may have a much healthier outlook after 30 days (or more) in treatment, and be better prepared to consider their own need for forgiveness through a relationship with Jesus Christ.

Dual Diagnoses Component

Many addicts struggle with one or more ancillary health conditions besides their addiction. If your loved one, in addition to their addiction, has one or more conditions that can trigger self-medication with alcohol or drugs, it would be wise, when evaluating rehabs, to make certain the program or facility has the staff and resources to treat all their conditions.

Besides his addiction, Chris struggled with debilitating anxiety, which at times was so severe he couldn't drive or keep food in his stomach. He underwent years of counseling and was prescribed medication, but he would regularly self-medicate with alcohol for relief. Which is why treatment for both addiction and anxiety were key considerations each time we evaluated rehabs. No one could tell us definitively which condition triggered the other (they probably both did), but it's noteworthy that Chris's anxiety disappeared altogether once he achieved long-term sobriety.

Loved Ones' Participation and Support

Most inpatient (or residential) rehabs encourage family involvement, which can be an integral factor to an addict's success. Each rehab has its own policy on when and how often you can communicate with and visit your loved one while in treatment. It's also common for rehabs to offer programs for loved ones of addicts, which provide education about addiction, the recovery process, and codependency.

We'll explore additional considerations for selecting a rehab in the next chapter.

TAKEAWAY:

Encourage your loved one to select a rehab that not only treats their substance addiction, but any secondary conditions—such as mood or eating disorders, anxiety, obsessing, etc.—which may trigger a relapse. Understand the role family would play at every rehab being considered. And evaluate your loved one's receptiveness to entering a faith-based versus secular treatment program.

GOD'S WORD:

"The beginning of wisdom is this: Get wisdom. Though it cost all you have, get understanding" (Proverbs 4:7, NIV).

PRAYER:

Lord, when the time comes to select a rehab for our loved ones, please guide us in selecting one that will help lead them to a life of sobriety.

Amen.

QUESTIONS:

1. Has your loved one ever been in rehab before? Was it successful? If not, why not?

2. Would your loved one be receptive to entering a faith-based rehab? What makes you think so?

3. Are there other health conditions besides addiction that your loved one needs treatment for in rehab?

Day 20:

Stop Selecting the Wrong Rehab Part 2

"For the Lord gives wisdom; from his mouth
come knowledge and understanding"
(Proverbs 2:6, NIV).

One night the Lord appeared to Solomon in a dream and said, "Ask for whatever you want me to give you" (1 Kings 3:5, NIV). Solomon replied, " ... give your servant a discerning heart to govern your people and to distinguish between right and wrong" (v.9). To which God replied, "I will give you a wise and discerning heart ..." (v.12).

All wisdom comes from God. And yet Solomon, a man who already possessed great wisdom, sought even more from the Lord. Shouldn't we desire the same—especially as it pertains to selecting the best rehab for our loved ones?

One of the biggest predictors of an addict's potential for success in rehab is their attitude prior to treatment. Why are they going? Do they even acknowledge their addiction? How badly do they want sobriety?

An Addict's Likelihood of Rehab Success

Is your loved one's attitude toward rehab reflected by any of the attitudes listed below?

- AGGRAVATION (low likelihood):
  "I'm only going to rehab to satisfy a court order and avoid jail. It's an utter waste of time."

- <u>RESIGNATION</u> (low to medium likelihood):
  "I'm only going to rehab to appease family and friends who think I have an addiction problem...which I don't."

- <u>MODERATION</u> (medium likelihood):
  "I'm going to rehab for help getting my binge drinking under control, so I can be more of a social drinker like my friends."

- <u>DESPERATION</u> (high likelihood):
  "Nothing is more important to me than achieving sobriety. Unless I get sober, nothing else that matters to me—such as my personal happiness, committed relationships, a successful career, and financial security—will likely ever happen."

Is your loved one desperate to escape the circumstances of their addiction? Then let's consider some other factors in determining which type of rehab would provide them the highest probability of success.

Inpatient Versus Outpatient Rehab

The chart below provides an excellent comparison between inpatient and outpatient rehabs:

Inpatient Rehab	Outpatient Rehab
1. Patient stays in the facility	1. Patient stays at home, but goes to treatment during the day
2. Higher success rate	
3. More expensive	
4. Disruptive to daily life	2. Lower success rate
5. 24-hour medical and emotional support	3. More affordable
	4. Patient maintains a more normal daily routine
6. 28 days to six month programs (or longer)	
7. Designed to treat serious addictions	5. Accessible to social circle support
8. No distractions of everyday life	6. 3 months to over a year program
	7. Good for someone with a mild addiction
	8. 10 to 12 hours a week

(Hayashida, Nov 1, 1998) (Inpatient vs. Outpatient Rehab, n.d.)

Someone new to an inpatient rehab program will be given an assessment and undergo a medically assisted detox (if necessary) to provide a safe withdrawal from alcohol and/or drugs. New patients (or "clients" as they are often called) will also receive assistance in dealing with drug or alcohol cravings during their detox, which might otherwise lead to relapse.

Inpatient rehabs generally cost more than outpatient programs, due to the 24-hour medical care and psychotherapy that is typically included. They are more effective options for loved ones with serious addictions who are experiencing difficulty coping or functioning, and who pose a danger to themselves and others.

Those with less active addictions can consider outpatient rehab, which could be supplemented by 12-step groups like Celebrate Recovery (Christ-centered), Narcotics Anonymous, or Alcoholics Anonymous.

Both inpatient and outpatient rehabs provide alcohol and drug abuse education, plus individual and group (facilitated) counseling. But don't assume this is the case. Always ask any prospective rehab center to provide detailed explanations of their programs.

Length of Inpatient Rehabs

Many addicts entering inpatient rehabs will only consider 30-day programs, as anything longer seems an untenable disruption to their lives. However, by the end of 30 days, a surprising percentage of patients—after being fully detoxed, educated, and counseled on their addiction—are far more receptive to extending the length of their treatment to fortify their sobriety.

This possible eventuality should be considered when selecting an inpatient rehab. Look for one that has multiple-length programs, which shorter-term patients can transition into.

Interpreting Success Rates

It's important to evaluate the success rate of any prospective rehab you are considering. But be wary of using success rates to compare one rehab to another. Since there's no standardization in the criteria used by rehabs in determining their success, it often becomes difficult to compare their relative effectiveness. For example, some rehabs base their success on the percentage of patients who graduate from their program; others base it on the percentage of patients who maintain their sobriety in the months and years following their graduation. It becomes apples and oranges.

Questions to Ask

Once you find a rehab that satisfies your needs on paper, schedule a visit to meet with the staff. Come prepared with a list of questions that address: accreditation and licensing; staff credentials and licensing; gender-specific programs; success rates (and how they define them); insurance compatibility; length of programs; patient-to-counselor ratios; and what role family plays.

Halfway (or Sober Living) Houses

Not all addicts have a safe home to return to following successful completion of a treatment program. Their home environment may contain triggers or be lacking a strong support system—thus creating the real potential for relapse. Or perhaps an addict's newfound sobriety is overwhelming, and requires a more gradual transition for reintegrating into society.

For such individuals who need help getting back on their feet, a halfway or sober living house is a great option. Typical costs range from $100 to $300 per month to over $2,000 per month. Length of stays range between three to twelve months—or however long is necessary to find a secure job (or start a school program) and feel confident in one's sobriety.

Virtually all halfway or sober houses have a list of rules and guidelines that residents must follow.

Common Guidelines for Residents of Halfway or Sober Houses

- You must stay sober. Drug and alcohol use is not allowed, and you're subject to random testing.

- You must contribute to the house by doing chores.

- No fighting or violence toward other residents.

- No stealing or destroying another resident's property.

- You must adhere to a curfew.

- You must attend 12-step or other recovery meetings.

- You may be required to interview for jobs if you don't already have one.

(Recovery Village, 2020)

Your loved one's rehab or treatment center will have recommendations on halfway or sober houses in your area.

TAKEAWAY:

Assess your loved one's likelihood of success for completing a rehab program. Then evaluate prospective rehabs by comparing their inpatient versus outpatient programs, program durations, ability to treat dual-diagnosis conditions, and so forth. Always have a plan for where your loved one will live once they complete rehab, especially if that might be a halfway or sober house.

GOD'S WORD:

"The fear of the Lord is the beginning of knowledge, but fools despise wisdom and instruction" (Proverbs 1:7, NIV).

PRAYER:

Heavenly Father, once our loved ones have entered rehab, help them be willing to extend the length of their program, if needed, to increase their chances for sobriety.

Amen.

QUESTIONS:

1. In reviewing "An Addict's Likelihood of Rehab Success," which stage do you think your loved one is in: Aggravation, Resignation, Moderation, or Desperation? As such, what is your current expectation of them being successful in rehab?

2. Considering the length and severity of your loved one's addiction, would an inpatient or outpatient rehab be most effective? What factors will go into making the decision?

3. How resistant do you think your loved one would be to extending their inpatient stay in rehab beyond the customary 30 days?

4. For your loved one, what are the three most important factors to consider when evaluating rehabs? Why?

Day 21:

Start Trusting—*Really Trusting*—God!

"Trust in the Lord with all your heart and lean not on your own understanding; in all your ways submit to him, and he will make your paths straight"
(Proverbs 3:5-6, NIV).

To be honest, I hesitated to include this chapter in my book. As transparent as I've tried to be about Chris's addiction, some incidents were just too painful and personal to relive. Nonetheless, I sense the Lord wanting me to share one such episode with you.

It occurred during the early morning hours of April 2nd, 2014. Chris was living in a small apartment about 30-minutes from my home.

Chris's mother and I, along with our daughter, strongly suspected (or in my case, fully believed) that he had expired in his apartment—the result of consuming more than a half-liter of vodka (about 11 1-1/2 ounce shots) and an unknown quantity of prescription drugs in a 24-hour period. He had been severely depressed and binge-drinking for about a week, and he wasn't responding to phone calls or text messages from family, friends, or his employer.

Convinced that Chris had passed, I became overwrought with crushing grief—sadly, something I've been no stranger to in life. Aside from grieving the loss of my parents and sister, I've endured the passing of four dear friends who separately made the same decision to take their own life. But none of those experiences prepared me for the grief I experienced that particular morning.

While driving to Chris's apartment, I was reminded of something my therapist told me years earlier, which I referenced in a previous chapter. He said if he had a 100 clients like Chris, he would expect only a few to survive. While you may think it was horribly cruel of him to say such a thing, he was wisely preparing me for the possibility of life without Chris. So in driving to Chris's apartment that morning, I was convinced that much-dreaded day had finally arrived.

I began to think what the next few days would look like. Notifying family members ... making service arrangements ... writing a eulogy ... selecting a burial plot. It all felt so surreal.

With tears streaming down my cheeks, I began to wonder: *Was there something more I could have done? Could I have stopped this, somehow? If not, then why didn't God?*

I began to recite Scripture that I had memorized many years earlier:

"Do not be anxious about anything, but in every situation, by prayer and petition, with thanksgiving, present your requests to God. And the peace of God, which transcends all understanding, will guard your hearts and your minds in Christ Jesus" (Philippians 4:6-7, NIV).

"You will keep in perfect peace those whose minds are steadfast, because they trust in you" (Isaiah 26:3, NIV).

"The Lord is close to the brokenhearted and saves those who are crushed in spirit (Psalm 34:18, NIV).

And the opening verse of this chapter:

"Trust in the Lord with all your heart and lean not on your own understanding; in all your ways submit to him, and he will make your paths straight" (Proverbs 3:5, NIV).

The calming presence of the Holy Spirit immediately washed over me. And I knew at that moment that no matter how fierce the storm that awaited me, God would be there. Helping me. Loving me. Comforting me.

Upon arriving at Chris's apartment building, I pushed the outdoor security buzzer to his apartment. I pushed it again, and again, and again. No answer. Frankly, I didn't expect an answer because I thought I already knew what had happened. As I pressed the buzzer one last time, I was preparing to call 9-1-1 from my phone in my other hand. The police would come, gain access to his apartment, and I would begin the excruciating process of saying my final goodbyes.

But as I pressed the buzzer, a shadow appeared in my peripheral vision. When I turned to look, there, on the other side of the glass—barely upright and profoundly intoxicated— stood Chris. He was alive! Praise God!

My experience that day taught me this important lesson: TRUST GOD!

Oh sure, I already knew this, but only on a superficial level. I really only trusted God when things were going my way. I needed my trust to go deeper ... much, much deeper.

Would I feel the same way had my worst fears that morning come true? Indeed, I would. In both the good times and bad— *especially the bad*—God is there. His indwelling Spirit guides me, speaks to me, calms me, assures me. Day in and day out, I have an abiding sense of His loving presence. "It is no longer I who live, but Christ who lives in me" (Galatians 2:20, ESV).

How do I know this? Read again two of the verses I cited earlier. Only this time, read them aloud. And as you do, emphasize the bolded words.

*"Do not be anxious about **anything**, but in **every** situation, by prayer and petition, with thanksgiving, present your requests to God. And the peace of God, which transcends **all** understanding, **will** guard your hearts and your minds in Christ Jesus" (Philippians 4:6-7, NIV, emphasis added).*

*"Trust in the Lord with **all** your heart and lean not on your own understanding; in **all** your ways submit to him, and he **will** make your paths straight" (Proverbs 3:5, NIV, emphasis add).*

There's really no wiggle room in how to interpret these verses. You either trust God or you don't. In every situation or none. It's really that simple—an absolutely glorious truth! Embrace it today as you continue your journey.

Finally, dear friend, if you still struggle trusting God for the sobriety of your loved one, I offer the following quotation. It seems a fitting end to this chapter and book:

"If God could close the lion's mouth for Daniel,
Part the red seas for Moses,
Make the sun stand still for Joshua,
Open the prison for Peter,
Put a baby in the arms of Sarah, and
Raise Lazarus from the dead,
Then He can certainly take care of you!
NOTHING you are facing today is too
hard for Him to handle!"

Author unknown

TAKEAWAY:

Morning and night, in both the good times and bad—remember to TRUST GOD!

GOD'S WORD:

"When I am afraid, I put my trust in you. In God, whose word I praise—in God I trust and am not afraid" (Psalm 56:3-4, NIV).

PRAYER:

Lord Jesus, help us to trust you in all circumstances, especially when we are afraid for our loved ones. Keep our mind steadfastly on You, oh Lord, so that we may abide in Your peace that surpasses all understanding.

Amen.

QUESTIONS:

1. Has your loved one ever done something so terrible that it caused you to question whether God could be trusted with his sobriety?

2. Do you tend to only trust God when everything is going your way?

3. Are there Scriptural promises you've memorized that you draw on in times of trouble? If not, do you plan to memorize any soon?

Closing Thoughts

Thank you for allowing me to share my codependency story with you. I trust it has helped edify, inspire, and equip you to avoid enabling behavior that might otherwise prolong and worsen your loved one's addiction.

I also hope you've learned how to forgive your loved one, and can one day celebrate being reconciled with one another as you slowly rebuild mutual trust in your relationship.

As you prayerfully await your loved one to "come to their senses" (like the prodigal son eventually did) and embrace sobriety, remember that you can neither cure them of their addiction nor protect them from self-destructive behavior. Detach yourself from that responsibility by "letting go and letting God," prayerfully imploring Him to guide your loved one on the path to sobriety.

If you'd like to learn more about codependency, especially as it relates to loved ones of addicts, I encourage you to check my suggested reading page for a list of book titles I think you would find helpful.

Finally, I hope many of you will prayerfully consider starting a Loved Ones of Addicts support group in your church, home, or other suitable gathering place. See the chapter titled, "Starting a 'Loved Ones of Addicts' Support Group," which provides you with everything you'll need.

God bless you and your loved one. My prayers are with both of you.

Jon Sorenson, Author

A Message from Chris Sorenson

Thank you for reading my father's book, *Stop Prolonging Your Loved One's Addiction.* When he asked me to participate in this project, the decision was an easy one. If this book could help lessen the suffering of just one addict or loved one of an addict, then it had my enthusiastic support.

The stories on these pages accurately depict how long and painful the addiction journey can be—not only for addicts, but for loved ones of addicts, who are the focus of this book.

For 18 years, I was slave to a severe alcohol addiction. There were countless days I lost the will to live. But I thank God every day for delivering me from that slavery. At the time of this writing, I have enjoyed six incredible years of sobriety. During that time, I have mended nearly two decades worth of broken trust and fractured relationships with family members and friends. Today I enjoy a life I could never have imagined in my darkest hours.

If you are anguishing over a loved one's addiction, I fervently pray you will find hope and comfort from this book. The miracle of sobriety is within reach of your loved one. But they must want it badly enough to do the necessary work that it requires, and to have faith that God has a plan—a wonderful plan—for their life.

I am so honored to be a part of this endeavor. I am proud and grateful for my dad who wrote it, and thankful to both my parents for never giving up on me.

God bless!

Starting a "Loved Ones of Addicts" Support Group

Leader's Support Group Meeting Guide

Promote Your Group

Three to four weeks before the first meeting of your group, post an announcement in your church bulletin, local newspaper, and via social media. Example:

"Loved Ones of Addicts" Support Group Forming

This 10-week confidential group is for anyone struggling with a loved one's drug or alcohol addiction. Each week we will read a chapter from "Stop Prolonging Your Loved One's Addiction," discuss its contents, share how we are doing, and pray for one another and our loved ones. [Provide dates, time, contact information, and how to register.]

Meeting Preparation

- Meeting length: 75-90 minutes.

- Arrive 5-10 minutes before the start of the meeting.

- Arrange chairs in a circle.

- Place a stapled copy of the Small Group Guidelines and The Serenity Prayer on each chair. (You can ask for them to be returned at the conclusion of the meeting so they can be reused.)

- As attendees arrive, warmly welcome each person and provide them with a nametag displaying their first name to wear somewhere prominent.

Meeting Format

Start the Meeting:
"Good evening, everyone! Welcome to the 'Loved Ones of Addicts' Support Group. My name is [your name] and I'll be your group facilitator. Let's open in prayer."

Lead the attendees in a short prayer asking God's protection for their loved ones, and that during the meeting He would make His presence known by speaking to the hearts of those in attendance.

Reading the Small Group Guidelines:
I suggest reading the entire guidelines during the group's first meeting. Thereafter, read only the bolded copy aloud and encourage new attendees to read them in their entirety. (Refer to separate sheet, "Loved Ones of Addicts" Support Group Guidelines.)

Brief Introductions:
"At this time, I'd like to give everyone an opportunity to tell the group your first name, and in one or two sentences, share what it is that brought you to group tonight. You'll have an opportunity to share more fully after our reading. If you prefer not to share, just say, 'Pass.' I'll start."

Your introduction should sound something like this: "My name is [first name] and I struggle with my [friend's, wife's, husband's, sister's, etc.] addiction to [alcohol or drugs]."

Encourage attendees to reply after each person's introduction by saying, "Hi, [the person's first name]."

Book Reading:
Following the introductions, read a chapter from "Stop Prolonging Your Loved One's Addiction," including the Support Group Questions at the end. If you're not a particularly good reader, feel free to ask someone else to do it.

Sharing Time:
"Now we'll transition into our sharing time, when each of you will have an opportunity, if you wish, to share with the group. Begin by selecting and answering any one of the Support Group Questions we just read, and then share what's happening in your life as it relates to your loved one. We suggest taking one minute to answer the Support Group Question you've selected, and two to three minutes to share about yourself. As always, if you prefer for any reason not to share, just say 'Pass.' Who would like to go first?"

Music:
Playing an uplifting and worshipful song that glorifies our Lord creates a perfect bridge from your sharing time to closing prayer.

Closing Prayer:
Once the sharing (and music) time ends, pray for the attendees and their loved ones. End the meeting by leading everyone in reading the Serenity Prayer. (Refer to separate sheet titled, "Serenity Prayer.")

"Loved Ones of Addicts" Support Group Guidelines

Follow these guidelines to ensure your support group is a safe place for everyone:

1. **Focus on your own thoughts and feelings when sharing.** Share your own feelings and personal experiences without disparaging others. Use sentences focusing on "I" or "me," not "you" or "we."

    Try limiting your sharing to three to five minutes. That way everyone will have an opportunity to share (if they wish), without any one person dominating the group sharing time.

2. **Do not engage in separate conversations with other group members while someone is sharing.**
    Each person should have the courtesy of sharing his or her feelings without being interrupted and distracted by others.

3. **The purpose of our group is to provide support for one another without trying to "fix" one another.** Because we are not licensed counselors, therapists, or psychologists, we should not dispense advice, attempt to solve other people's problems, or refer people to counselors. It is incumbent on each participant to pursue outside counseling if they feel the need for professional help.

4. **Whatever is shared in the group should stay in the group. Every participant is entitled to complete anonymity and confidentiality.*** Nothing that is shared in the group should ever be discussed with any other person, including a spouse, family member, co-worker, etc.

    *The only exception is if someone threatens to injure themselves or others. If this happens, it will be reported to the proper authorities.

5. **Offensive language is prohibited.**
    This includes using the Lord's name inappropriately, other crude language, and any use of graphic/explicit descriptions.

    Please note the Guidelines remain in force even when participants fellowship with one another after the meeting.

Serenity Prayer

by Reinhold Niebuhr
(1892 – 1971)

God, grant me the serenity
To accept the things I cannot change,
The courage to change the things I can,
And the wisdom to know the difference.
Living one day at a time,
Enjoying one moment at a time,
Accepting hardship as a pathway to peace,
Taking, as Jesus did, this sinful world as it is,
Not as I would have it;
Trusting that You will make all things right
If I surrender to Your will;
So that I may be reasonably happy in this life,
And supremely happy with You,
Forever in the next.

Amen.

Suggested Reading

Boundaries – Dr. Henry Cloud & Dr. John Townsend
Codependent No More – Melody Beattie

Codependents' Guide to the Twelve Steps – Melody Beattie

The Language of Letting Go: Daily Meditations on Codependency – Melody Beattie

One Day at a Time in Al-Anon – Al-Anon

Courage to Change: One Day at a Time II – Al-Anon

Addict in the Family: Stories of Loss, Hope, and Recovery – Beverly Conyers

Everything Changes: Help for Families of Newly Recovering Addicts – Beverly Conyers

Praying for Your Addicted Loved One: 90 in 90 – Sharron K. Cosby

When Someone You Love Abuses Drugs or Alcohol – Cecil Murphey

About the Author

 Jon Sorenson was born and raised in small-town Minnesota. He became a follower of Jesus Christ at age 11 after receiving the gift of salvation while watching a televised Billy Graham crusade. He is retired from a career that included 25 years in sales and marketing, and 15 years directing communications for a 4,200-person church in suburban Minneapolis. Jon and his wife, Nancie, currently reside in a suburb of the Twin Cities in close proximity to their three adult children, three grandchildren, and one highly spoiled dog, "Simba."

MEDIA AND CONTACT INFO:

Facebook: Jon's Facebook Group ("Loved Ones of Addicts | Faith-Based") is a Christian community comprised of individuals who struggle with a loved one's addiction. Members receive prayer support, uplifting Scripture, and codependency education. Join the group at: www.facebook.com/groups/LOOAGroup

Website: www.LovedOnesOfAddicts.org

Contact: looa.faithbased@gmail.com

References

Al-Anon Meetings. (n.d.). Retrieved April 5, 2020, from Al-Anon: www.al-anon.org/al-anon-meetings

Comparison of Relapse Rates Between Substance Use Disorders and Other Chronic Illnesses. (2000). Journal of the American Medical Association (JAMA).

Elkins, C. (n.d.). Relapse & Slips: Warning Signs, Triggers & Prevention Plan. Retrieved from www.drugrehab.com: www.drugrehab.com/recovery/relapse

Hayashida, M. M. (Nov 1, 1998). An Overview of Outpatient and Inpatient Detoxification. Alcohol Health and Research World, Vol 22.

Inpatient vs. Outpatient Rehab. (n.d.). Retrieved April 6, 2020, from AddictionCenter: www.addictioncenter.com/treatment/inpatient-outpatient-rehab

Lennon, J. (1980).

Marlatt, G. A. and Donovan, D. M. (2005). Relapse Prevention.

Melemis, S.M. (Sept 1988). Relapse Prevention and the Five Rules of Recovery. *Yale Journal of Biology and Medicine, 325-332.*

Recovery Village. (2020, February 6). What is a Halfway House and Why Should You Consider It? Retrieved April 6, 2020, from The Recovery Village: www.therecoveryvillage.com/treatment-program/aftercare/faq/what-is-a-halfway-house

Resources for Professionals. (n.d.). Retrieved April 5, 2020, from Al-Anon: www.al-anon.org/resources-for-professionals

Made in United States
Cleveland, OH
21 February 2025

14570258R00094